Nursing Home Survival Guide

By

EVAN H. FARR

CERTIFIED ELDER LAW ATTORNEY

*Helping You Protect
Your Loved Ones Who
Need Nursing Home Care
by Preserving Dignity,
Quality of Life, and
Financial Security*

Library of Congress Control Number: 2012922727

ISBN 978-0976182122

First Printing April 2013

Published by
Quality Legal Publications, LLC
Fairfax, Virginia

Quality Legal
Publications

This book provides general legal information only. Although the legal information contained in this publication is believed to be accurate at the time of publication, no guarantee of accuracy is made by the publisher or the author. Laws develop over time, change frequently, and differ from state to state. This book cannot and does not provide legal advice about specific legal problems or situations. If legal advice is required, the service of an experienced attorney should be sought.

Printed in the United States of America

Dedicated to my clients and co-workers at the
Farr Law Firm, without whom this book
would not be possible.

TABLE OF CONTENTS

PREFACE - THE FINAL MOVE

It was Benjamin Franklin who gave us the still-famous and oft-quoted saying about death and taxes. In a letter to a friend, Ben wrote:

> "Our new Constitution is now established, and has an appearance that promises permanency; but in this world nothing can be said to be certain, except death and taxes."

When Ben wrote these words in 1789, the average life expectancy in America was only 35 years old. Although the United States Constitution has been amended 27 times since then, this noble document that Ben helped write has indeed held up pretty well for a document that's now more than 220 years old.

And the United States of America that Ben helped create has also held up pretty well over all those years. So well, in fact, that American life expectancy has continued to increase over the decades. According to the U.S. Census Bureau, at the turn of the 20th century, the average life expectancy had increased from 35 to approximately 47, and 100 years later, at the turn our current 21st century, average life expectancy had increased to approximately 77, with approximately 17 percent of the American population living past age 85.

And because of this increase in life expectancy, the percentage of older Americans continues to rise as well. As of 2009, according to the Census Bureau, 12.9 percent of the population – approximately one out of every eight Americans – were age 65 or older, compared to one in 10 in the 1950s.

In 2011, the Baby Boomers (those born between 1946 and 1964) started turning 65. According to the Federal Interagency Forum on Aging-Related Statistics (AgingStats.gov), the number of older adults will increase dramatically over the next 20 years – they project that the older population in the year 2030 will be more than **double** what it was in 2000, growing from 35 million to 71.5 million and representing nearly 20 percent of the total U.S. population.

On top of this drastic aging of America, consider the following statistics:

- About 70 percent of Americans who live to age 65 will need long-term care at some time in their lives, over 40 percent in a nursing home.

- As of 2012, the national average cost of a private room in a nursing home was $248 per day, or $90,520 per year, and the national average cost of a semi-private room was $222 per day, or $81,030 per year.

- On average, someone age 65 today will need long-term care services for three years, women averaging longer than men. Twenty percent of Americans will need long-term care for more than five years.

- Long-term care is not just needed by the elderly. A study by Unum, released in November 2008, found that 46 percent of its group long-term care claimants were under the age of 65 at the time of disability.

As a result of the aging of our population and the fact that Americans are living longer and longer, more and more Americans are developing chronic illnesses that require long-term care, and we all face increasingly difficult challenges and more transitions in our lives than ever before. One of the most difficult transitions that Americans must face for themselves and/or their loved ones is the "final move" – a transition that's made by over 40% of the American population – the move to a nursing home.

This last transition often happens gradually – perhaps your loved one has suffered for years with a degenerative chronic illness and has progressed through in-home care to an assisted living facility, and now needs the type of care that can only be provided in a nursing home. Or perhaps the need for the final move comes suddenly – necessitated by a major health event such as a stroke, a heart attack, or a broken hip, or by some other health event common in the elderly, such as dehydration or a urinary tract infection. Whatever the reason, the final move during a time of great stress.

Whether moving to a nursing facility directly from a private home or other independent living arrangement, or from an assisted living facility, or after a hospital stay, the final move is almost always emotionally gut-wrenching and can be devastatingly traumatic – for both the nursing home resident and for the family member(s) involved with the decision to make this final move.

There are innumerable reasons why this final move is so difficult. For some, the final move involves the loss of a home (often a home with a lifetime of memories). For many, the final move means the loss of privacy, because most nursing home beds are in double rooms. For all, the final move means a total loss of independence.

The spouse or relative who helps a loved one transition into a nursing home faces the immediate dilemma of how to find the right nursing home. The task is no small one, and a huge sigh of relief can be heard if and when the right home is found and the loved one is moved into the nursing home. But for many, the most difficult task is just beginning: how to cope with nursing home bills that may total $8,000 to $12,000 per month or more?

Rich, poor, or somewhere in between, 99 percent of Americans can't afford to ignore the potentially catastrophic costs of nursing home care and other types of long-term care, such as assisted living and in-home care. In fact, long-term care costs are so high that 70 percent of Americans become impoverished within a year of entering a nursing home. Chances are that someone close to you has lost their dignity and their life savings by winding up broke in a nursing home.

This Nursing Home Survival Guide is designed to provide much-needed information and answers to the important questions you will encounter as you go through this challenging transition. These are questions that I, as a Certified Elder Law Attorney, deal with on a daily basis. It is my sincere hope that this book will be of valuable assistance to you. Let's start with some basic definitions . . .

Evan H. Farr, CELA
Certified as an Elder Law Attorney by the National Elder Law Foundation
Creator of the Living Trust Plus™:   http://www.LivingTrustPlus.com
Farr Law Firm, 10640 Main Street, Suite 200, Fairfax, VA 22030
VirginiaElderLaw.com   &   VirginiaEstatePlanning.com
Daily Blog: blog.EverythingElderLaw.com
Weekly Blog: blog.ElderLawPlus.com
703-691-1888 or 1-800-399-FARR

chapter 1

WHAT IS A NURSING HOME?

Nursing homes have only been around since the 1950s, but most likely you or someone close to you has spent time in a nursing home. Over the past several decades, nursing homes have become big business. The vast majority of all nursing homes are for-profit entities, and many of these are large corporations with nursing facilities in multiple states. Nursing homes generally provide three types of services:

- rehabilitation for people who are injured, sick, or disabled;

- skilled nursing and medical care;

- custodial care (help with eating, dressing, bathing, toileting, and moving about).

Like hospitals, nursing homes never close — service must be available 24 hours a day, 365 days a year with trained, licensed nursing staff always present. A nursing facility is required to maintain interdisciplinary staffing at several levels, including licensed nursing facility administrators and physician medical directors, directors of nursing services, nurses trained to provide skilled nursing care, social workers, and activities directors. They are also required to hire as staff or retain as consultants:

- A pharmacist;

- Therapists in a variety of specialties, including physical, occupational and speech therapy;

- Food service personnel, including a dietary supervisor; and

- An interdisciplinary assessment and assurance committee.

Nursing facilities must be licensed under state law as nursing facilities. Assisted Living facilities are not nursing homes. More than 80% of nursing homes also choose to participate in Medicare and Medicaid, which require nursing homes to meet strict federal certification standards on quality of care, quality of life, and residents' rights. For the purposes of this book and in general consumer usage, all licensed nursing facilities are considered skilled care facilities. However, the federal government refers to non-Medicare-certified facilities as "nursing facilities" and to Medicare-certified facilities as "skilled nursing facilities" or "SNFs."

> *A nursing home must be licensed under state law as a nursing home. Assisted Living facilities are not nursing homes.*

Either an entire facility or a portion of a facility can be licensed as a nursing facility. Continuing Care Retirement Communities (CCRC) and Life Care Communities (LCC) offer skilled nursing facility services for their residents. Some hospitals may also provide skilled nursing care in a long-term care unit.

Nursing facilities use personnel at a variety of training levels, which allows patient care needs to be matched to appropriate training levels. Licensed nursing care levels include: Licensed Practical Nurse (LPN); Registered Nurse (RN); Clinical Nurse Specialist (CNS); and Registered Nurse Practitioner (RNP).

In addition to the types of licensed and registered nurses listed above, almost all nursing facilities make heavy use of CNAs, (Certified Nurse Assistants or Certified Nurse Aides), to provide most of the day-to-day basic services provided in a nursing home. CNAs may provide assistance with Activities of Daily Living (ADLs) such as bathing, dressing, eating, toileting, transferring, and bowel/bladder incontinence, as well as assistance with Instrumental ADLs (IADLs) which include housekeeping duties such as laundry and meal preparation. In general, CNAs must have a high school diploma or GED, and must have completed a 6-to-12 week CNA certification program at a community college or medical facility. Classroom instruction in a certified nursing assistant program generally includes: basic nursing skills, anatomy and physiology, nutrition, and infection control. Regulations on nursing assistant certification vary from state-to-state.

NURSING HOME GOALS

The goals of all nursing facilities are to: (1) rehabilitate the resident to maximum potential and enable the resident to return to independent living arrangements if possible; (2) maintain maximum rehabilitation as long as possible within the realities of age and disease; (3) delay deterioration in physical and emotional well-being; and (4) support the resident and family, physically and emotionally, when health declines to the point of death. Nursing homes that receive federal funds must comply with federal legislation that calls for a high quality of care. Though all states must comply, at a minimum, with the federal regulations, some states have adopted tougher laws.

> *Nursing homes must provide* services and activities to attain or maintain the highest practicable physical, mental, and psychosocial well-being of each resident in accordance with a written plan of care.

Congress enacted legislation in 1987 requiring nursing homes participating in the Medicare and Medicaid programs to comply with certain requirements for quality of care. This federal law, known as the Nursing Home Reform Act, specifies that a nursing home "must provide services and activities to attain or maintain the highest practicable physical, mental, and psychosocial well-being of each resident in accordance with a written plan of care. ...."

To participate in the Medicare and Medicaid programs, nursing homes must:

3

- Have sufficient nursing staff. (42 CFR §483.30)

- Conduct initially a comprehensive and accurate assessment of each resident's functional capacity. (42 CFR §483.20)

- Develop a comprehensive care plan for each resident. (42 CFR §483.20)

- Prevent the deterioration of a resident's ability to bathe, dress, groom, transfer and ambulate, toilet, eat, and to communicate. (42 CFR §483.25)

- Provide, if a resident is unable to carry out activities of daily living, the necessary services to maintain good nutrition, grooming, and personal oral hygiene. (42 CFR §483.25)

- Ensure that residents receive proper treatment and assistive devices to maintain vision and hearing abilities. (42 CFR §483.25)

- Ensure that residents do not develop pressure sores and, if a resident has pressure sores, provide the necessary treatment and services to promote healing, prevent infection, and prevent new sores from developing. (42 CFR §483.25)

- Provide appropriate treatment and services to incontinent residents to restore as much normal bladder functioning as possible. (42 CFR §483.25)

- Ensure that the resident receives adequate supervision and assistive devices to prevent accidents. (42 CFR §483.25)

- Maintain acceptable parameters of nutritional status. (42 CFR §483.25)

- Provide each resident with sufficient fluid intake to maintain proper hydration and health. (42 CFR §483.25)

- Ensure that residents are free of any significant medication errors. (42 CFR §483.25)

- Promote each resident's quality of life. (42 CFR §483.15)

- Maintain dignity and respect of each resident. (42 CFR §483.15)

- Ensure that the resident has the right to choose activities, schedules, and health care. (42 CFR §483.40)

- Provide pharmaceutical services to meet the needs of each resident. (42 CFR §483.60)

- Be administered in a manner that enables it [the nursing home] to use its resources effectively and efficiently. (42 CFR §483.75)

- Maintain accurate, complete, and easily accessible clinical records on each resident (42 CFR §483.75)

chapter 2

WHAT IS LONG-TERM CARE?

A ccording the American healthcare system, long-term care differs from health care in that the goal of long-term care is not to cure an illness, but to allow an individual to attain and maintain an optimal level of functioning. Long-term care encompasses a wide array of medical, social, personal, and supportive and specialized housing services needed by individuals who have lost some capacity for self-care because of a chronic illness or disabling condition.

Long-term care encompasses a broad continuum of care:

> *According the American healthcare system, long-term care differs from health care in that the goal of long-term care is not to cure an illness, but to allow an individual to attain and maintain an optimal level of functioning.*

- Long-term care may involve medical care or skilled nursing care;

- Long-term care most often involves "intermediate care" or "custodial care" – the type of care where people received assistance with "Activities of Daily Living" (toileting, bathing, dressing, eating, walking, transferring) or "Instrumental Activities of Daily Living (things such as shopping, cooking, household chores, care of pets, and financial management)."

- Long-term care often involves supervision due to Alzheimer's disease or other forms of dementia.

WHERE IS LONG-TERM CARE PROVIDED?

- **At Home.** Home health care is provided in an individual's home (by family members or paid staff) and aims to keep the individual functioning at the highest possible level. Services range from basic assistance with household chores to skilled nursing services.

- **Assisted Living Facilities**. An Assisted Living Facility (ALF) typically provides apartment-style accommodations where services focus on providing assistance with ADLs and IADLs, including meals, housekeeping, medication assistance, laundry, and regular check-ins. Designed to bridge the gap between independent living and nursing home care.

- **Nursing Homes.** As already explained, a nursing home is a medical facility that provides 24-hour nursing care for people with serious illnesses or disabilities. The vast majority of all nursing homes are for-profit entities, and many of these are large corporations with nursing facilities in multiple states. Nursing homes generally provide three levels of service:

- **Adult Day Care.** Adult day care programs provide meals and care services in a community setting during the day while a caregiver needs time off or must work.

- **Continuing Care Retirement Communities** (CCRC) or **Life Care Communities** (LCC). CCRCs or LCCs provide a continuum of care from independent living through skilled nursing. The facilities allow individuals to live within the same community as their needs progress through the spectrum of care.

chapter 3

THE DOUBLE TRAGEDY OF CHRONIC ILLNESS

A chronic illness is a disease that is long-lasting or recurrent, and needs to be managed on a long-term basis. According to various reports published by the Robert Wood Johnson Foundation, almost half of all Americans (roughly 150 million people) live with chronic illness, and people with chronic illness account for 83 percent of health care spending.

According to the National Center for Chronic Disease Prevention and Health Promotion, part of the Centers for Disease Control and Prevention, chronic diseases – such as heart disease, diabetes, and arthritis – are among the most common, costly, and preventable of all health problems in the U.S., and chronic illnesses such as these cause approximately 70% of deaths in the United States.

> *Our American health insurance system discriminates against people suffering from certain types of chronic illnesses, i.e., chronic illnesses that routinely result in the need for long-term care.*

According to a 2004 report by the Bloomberg School of Public Health at The Johns Hopkins University (analyzing data from 1998), 85% of seniors (over age 65) have at least one chronic disease, and 62% of them have two or more chronic illnesses. According to that same report, of adults between the ages of 18 and 64, 45% have at least one chronic disease, and 20% have two or more chronic illnesses.

WHY IS CHRONIC ILLNESS IMPORTANT?

The expenses of long-term care caused by a chronic illness are often catastrophic because Americans do not have a right to receive basic long-term care, and therefore wind up paying privately for most long-term care. Through Medicare, seniors have had virtually universal **health insurance** coverage for **most** chronic illnesses since 1965. For individuals under age 65, private health insurance has likewise always covered treatment, medication, and surgery for **most** chronic illnesses - such as heart disease, lung disease, kidney disease, and hundreds of other chronic medical conditions.

AMERICA'S HEALTH INSURANCE SYSTEM EFFECTIVELY DISCRIMINATES AGAINST CERTAIN CHRONIC ILLNESSES

The double tragedy of chronic illness is that our American health insurance system discriminates against people suffering from certain types of chronic illnesses, *i.e.*, those that routinely result in the need for long-term care, such as: Alzheimer's disease and other types of dementias; Parkinson's disease and other types of degenerative disorders of the central nervous system; Huntington's disease, Amytrophic Lateral Sclerosis (ALS), and other progressive neurodegencrative disorders; and many genetic disorders such as Multiple Sclerosis and Muscular Dystrophy. Those Americans suffering the tragedy of one of these diseases must also suffer the tragedy of having the "wrong" disease according to our American health insurance system. Is it an ethical social policy that seemingly arbitrarily distinguishes among these different types of illnesses? Is it an ethical social policy that provides full coverage for most illnesses – whether chronic or acute – but forces Americans with certain chronic conditions (many of them elders) to become impoverished in order to gain access to the long-term care necessitated by their particular type of chronic illness? Is it a surprise that Americans suffering the "wrong type" of chronic illness will want to look for legal ways to preserve the efforts of their lifetime in order to protect themselves from this unfair and seemingly arbitrary social policy?

chapter 4

THE CAREGIVER'S ROLE

I f you're reading this book, chances are good that you are either a caregiver, or are facing the possibility of becoming a caregiver. Maybe you've been caring for your disabled spouse, or perhaps your aging parent is beginning to show signs of dementia. You're probably struggling with all kinds of difficult questions. Chances are that the person you're caring for never made any real plans for what to do in the event of physical disability or dementia.

Most family members who help their older loved ones don't see themselves as caregivers. Yet a caregiver is anyone who helps an older person with household chores, errands, personal care,

> *A caregiver is anyone who helps an older person with household chores, errands, personal care, or finances.*

or finances. Most caregivers also don't realize that caring for themselves is an important part of providing care for someone else. The simple truth is you can't be a good caregiver if you don't take care of yourself.

If you have been taking care of your spouse, perhaps you are afraid of giving up the caregiver role, even if your own health may be deteriorating as a result of the stress of having to care for your spouse. If you are an adult child, perhaps you are worried about having to provide care for a parent with diminishing health and declining capacity. It is often very difficult for an adult child to step into a relationship reversal by taking over the parental role, but that is often exactly what happens — the child must become the parent, and the parent assumes the role of the child. This transition is fraught with conflict, confusion, and pain. If you're an adult child, most likely you have a career, children, and your own family and personal limitations to deal with. How can you possibly be expected to have to take care of your parents also?

Many conflicting thoughts and emotions arise when someone is confronted with having to care for an aging parent or a disabled spouse:

- **Love and Responsibility:** a desire to provide the best care for your spouse or for your parents.

- **Fear:** fear of losing your spouse or parent; fear of losing control; fear of the unknown; fear of not being able to conserve financial assets for future needs.

- **Confusion:** not knowing what long-term care options are available, how to get the best care, how much money will need to be spent on nursing care.

- **Guilt:** for not being able to do more for your spouse or parent.

- **Anger and Frustration:** over the fact that your spouse or parent failed to plan ahead and foresee that this day might come.

- **Resentment:** over why you are the one stuck being the primary caregiver.

- **Conflict:** constant arguments with a spouse or parent who has progressive dementia.

- **Self-preservation:** worry about how much of your own limited resources must be used to provide care for your spouse or parent.

All of these feelings are normal and are neither good nor bad. Give yourself a break; being a caregiver is hard, often underappreciated work. Negative feelings do not mean you love the person any less. Allow yourself to feel how you feel and forgive yourself for any negative feelings.

CAREGIVER STRESS TEST

Which of the following are seldom true, sometimes true, often true or usually true?

- I find I can't get enough rest.

- I don't have enough time for myself.

- I don't have enough time to be with family members other than the one I care for.

- I feel guilty about my situation.

- I don't get out much anymore.

- I have conflict with the person I take care of.

- I have conflicts with other family members.

- I cry a lot.

- I worry about having enough money to make ends meet.

- I don't feel I have enough knowledge or experience to give care as well as I'd like.

- I worry about my own health.

If the response to one or more or these areas is usually true or often true, it may be time to look for help with giving care and help with taking care of yourself.

> *Negative feelings do not mean you love the person any less. Allow yourself to feel how you feel and forgive yourself for any negative feelings.*

CAREGIVER BURNOUT

According to WebMD,[1] Caregiver Burnout is a state of physical, emotional, and mental exhaustion that may be accompanied by a change in attitude -- from positive and caring to negative and unconcerned. Burnout can occur when caregivers don't get the help they need, or if they try to do more than they are able -- either physically or financially. Caregivers who are "burned out" may experience fatigue, stress, anxiety, and depression.

Caregivers often are so busy caring for others that they tend to neglect their own emotional, physical, and spiritual health. The demands on a caregiver's body, mind, and emotions can easily seem overwhelming, leading to fatigue and hopelessness -- and, ultimately, burnout. Other factors that can lead to caregiver burnout include:

Role confusion -- you may be confused when thrust into the role of caregiver. It may be difficult for you to separate your role as caregiver from your role as spouse, lover, child, friend, etc.

Unrealistic expectations -- you may expect your involvement to have a positive effect on the health and happiness of the patient. This may be unrealistic for patients suffering from a progressive disease, such as Parkinson's or Alzheimer's.

Lack of control -- you may become frustrated by a lack of money, resources, and skills to effectively plan, manage, and organize your loved one's care.

Unreasonable demands -- you may place unreasonable burdens on yourself, in part because you see providing care as your exclusive responsibility.

---

[1] http://women.webmd.com/caregiver-recognizing-burnout

Other factors -- You may not recognize when you are suffering burnout and eventually get to the point where you cannot function effectively. You may even become sick yourself.

SYMPTOMS OF CAREGIVER BURNOUT

Again according to WebMD,[2] the symptoms of caregiver burnout are similar to the symptoms of stress and depression. They include:

- Withdrawal from friends, family and other loved ones.

- Loss of interest in activities previously enjoyed.

- Feeling blue, irritable, hopeless, and helpless.

- Changes in appetite, weight, or both.

- Changes in sleep patterns.

- Getting sick more often.

- Feelings of wanting to hurt yourself or the person for whom you are caring.

- Emotional and physical exhaustion.

- Irritability.

WHAT YOU CAN DO

Take charge of your life. Don't let your loved one's illness or disability always take center stage. While you might fall into a caregiving role because of an unexpected event, somewhere along the line you need to step back and consciously say "I choose to take on this caregiving role." It goes a long way toward eliminating the feeling of being a victim.

Set realistic goals. Caregiving creates many conflicting demands on your time; it is vital to set realistic goals. Recognize what you

---

[2] http://women.webmd.com/caregiver-recognizing-burnout

can and cannot do. Define your priorities and stick to them as much as you can. You have the right to set limits and, though it is hard, it is okay to say no.

Seek out help from family and friends. When others offer assistance, accept it and suggest specific things they can do. Some caregivers see asking for help as a sign of weakness, failure or inadequacy, when in fact it is just the opposite. Reaching out for assistance before you are beyond your limits is one characteristic of a strong person. While they might not be comfortable helping with bathing and dressing needs, friends and family can help by running errands, shopping for groceries, preparing meals or just visiting. They can call regularly, taking some pressure off you to be the primary social outlet.

Seek out appropriate geriatric medical professionals. A geriatrician is a medical doctor who is specially trained to prevent and manage the unique health concerns of older adults. Older persons may react to illness and disease differently than younger adults. Geriatricians are able to treat older patients, manage multiple disease symptoms, and develop care plans that address the special health care needs of older adults. Geriatricians are typically primary care physicians who are board-certified in either Family Practice or Internal Medicine and have also acquired the additional training necessary to obtain the Certificate of Added Qualifications in Geriatric Medicine. You can locate a geriatrician in your area through the Web site of either the American Medical Association (www.ama-assn.org) or the American Board of Family Medicine (www.theabfm.org).

Seek out the assistance of a Geriatric Care Manager. GCMs are professionals with degrees in one or more fields of human services (e.g., social work, psychology, nursing, or gerontology), who specialize in assisting older people and their families with long-term care arrangements. GCMs are typically independent from the resources they recommend, so they can provide an unbiased

15

assessment of each situation. GCMs can work with families and elders prior to the need for services and can also assist in emergency situations. You can locate a GCM in your area through the Web site of National Association of Professional Geriatric Care Managers at http://www.caremanager.org.

Investigate community and professional resources such as in-home health services or adult daycare. Employ a home health aide to cook, clean and help with bathing, eating, dressing, using the bathroom and getting around the house. Check your local phonebook under "Home Health Care Providers." These are the types of services that an older parent should expect to have to pay for if they are not available for free in the community.

When you just need a short break, consider respite care. You can hire a companion to stay with your care-receiver for a few hours at a time on a regular basis to give you some time off. In addition, most nursing homes and assisted living facilities offer families the opportunity to place older relatives in their facilities for short stays. Your local area's agency on aging can help with arrangements.

> *When you just need a short break, consider respite care. Most nursing homes and assisted living facilities offer families the opportunity to place older relatives in their facilities for short stays.*

chapter 5

SELECTING A FACILITY

Most nursing home admissions happen under a great deal of stress. There are generally two ways a nursing admission takes place – either directly from home to a nursing facility, or via discharge from a hospital to a nursing facility for short-term rehabilitation.

In order to get admitted directly from home to a nursing facility, a family member typically must call the local nursing facilities to determine if they have openings. Calling the local nursing facilities every day, first thing in the morning, is often the best way to find an opening. Even if a nursing facility says they will add your loved one to a waiting list, persistence in calling every day is often rewarded because if an opening is available, it is easier for the nursing home admission staff to say "come on over" rather than facing the prospect of calling down a waiting list and perhaps

A rehab discharge is the easier way of getting into a nursing home, and also has the advantage of the fact that this type of short-term rehabilitation will be covered primarily by Medicare

spending hours before finding someone who is ready to move in that day.

A rehabilitation (rehab) discharge occurs when an individual has been admitted to a hospital for an acute injury or illness, has remained hospitalized for at least 3 days, and is then transferred directly from the hospital to a nursing facility for short-term rehabilitation (physical therapy, speech therapy, etc.). Not only is this the easier way of getting into a nursing home, but it also has the advantage of the fact that this type of short-term rehabilitation will be covered primarily by Medicare. See page 36 for more information about Medicare-covered rehabilitation.

A rehab discharge often occurs with the assistance of a hospital "case manager" (sometimes called a "discharge planner"), who is typically a nurse or a social worker. Case managers have general information about nursing facilities near the hospital, but they normally don't have time to learn about the actual quality of care in a given facility. In some jurisdictions, there is an area-wide computer system whereby hospital case managers can simply send out a request to area nursing facilities to see which facility has an opening for the patient needing rehab.

> *It is easier, and better for your loved one, if the first placement is to the best possible facility. Although a nursing home resident can be moved from one facility to another, this type of disruption can be very disturbing and is rarely in everyone's best interest.*

Regardless of whether you are admitting your loved to a nursing facility directly from home or via a rehab discharge, you may be faced with the overwhelming task of finding the best nursing home for a loved one. It is easier, and better for your loved one, if the first placement is to the best possible facility. Although a nursing home resident can be moved from one facility to another, this type of disruption can be very disturbing and is rarely in everyone's best interest.

WHERE DO YOU BEGIN?

To get the best possible nursing home, the first step is for the family and/or potential resident to determine what is most important to them in looking for a facility. The resident's needs and desires must be included in this evaluation. Variables such as location of the facility, whether a special care unit is available, and what types of payment sources are accepted should also be considered when beginning this process.

The next step is to identify the facilities in your area which meet the criteria you have established. If placement is not urgent, you can contact each nursing facility in your nearby area and ask for its information packet, which should include an activity calendar and a menu. You should also ask for the three most recent state annual inspection reports detailing the facility's major and minor deficiencies; nursing homes are required to make these reports available upon request. Virtually every nursing home will have some deficiencies; after all, working with extremely disabled and impaired persons is very difficult. Your local Area Agency on Aging should also have resources and helpful aids for assisting you in finding and comparing nursing homes.

The most helpful of all resources is Medicare's Nursing Home Quality Compare Website at www.medicare.gov/NHCompare. Here, you can obtain detailed inspection

> *The most helpful of all resources is Medicare's Nursing Home Quality Compare Website at www.medicare.gov/NHCompare*

information about each nursing facility that interests you, comparing various government-rated "quality measures" such as: *Percent of Residents Who Have Moderate to Severe Pain, Percent of High-Risk Residents Who Have Pressure Sores, Percent of Residents Who Were Physically Restrained, and Percent of Residents Who Spend Most of Their Time in Bed or in a Chair.* The NHCompare Web site also rates the care and services that each facility provides to its residents, and allows you to view how each facility stacks up in staffing hours for each type of health care worker against state and national averages. The NHCompare Web site also tells you whether each facility accepts Medicare and Medicaid.

Step three is to tour the facilities you have identified in step two. Assuming you're interested in Medicaid Asset Protection, which will be discussed starting on page 66, then limit your search to those nursing homes that accept Medicaid, which is almost all nursing homes. There is no need to schedule your visits in advance (even though some nursing homes prefer this). Just show up during regular business hours. You should be able to meet with an administrative staff member, who should be able to answer all your questions. You will also want to tour a second time, in the evening or on the weekend, to see if there is a drastic difference in the atmosphere of the facility or the care being provided. It is important to tour at least two facilities so you can see the difference in the physical plant and the staff.

While you are touring the facility, pay attention to your gut feeling. Ask yourself:

- Do I feel welcome?

- How long did I have to wait to meet with someone?

- Did the admissions director ask about my family member's wants and needs?

- Is the facility clean?

- Are there any strong odors?

- Is the staff friendly?

- Do they seem to genuinely care for the residents?

- Do the staff seem to get along with each other?

Listen and observe. You can learn a lot just by watching and paying attention. And ask questions. You want to be sure that the facility is giving proactive care, not just reacting to crisis. Here are a few examples of the types of questions the staff should be able to answer:

- How do you ensure that call lights are answered promptly, regardless of your staffing?

- If my father is not able to move or turn himself, how do you ensure that he is turned and does not develop bedsores?

- How do you make sure that someone is assisted with the activities of daily living like dressing, toileting and transferring?

- Can residents bring in their own supplies?

- Can residents use any pharmacy they wish?

> Listen and observe. You can learn a lot just by watching and paying attention. And ask questions. You want to be sure that the facility is giving proactive care, not just reacting to crisis.

- How many direct care staff members do you have on each shift? Does this number exceed the minimal number that state regulations require, or do you just meet the minimum standard?

- What sources of payment do you accept?

- How long has the medical director been with your facility?

- How were your last state survey results? (Get a copy.)

- How did you correct any deficiencies and what process did you put in place to make sure you do not make these mistakes again?

- Has the state prohibited this facility from accepting new residents at any time during the last 2 years?

- What is your policy on family care planning conferences? Will you adjust your schedule to make sure that I can attend the meeting?

- Do you have a list of references I can talk with?

- Can my loved one come in for a meal to see if he/she fits in and likes the facility?

Beginning on page 24, you will find a comprehensive Nursing Home Evaluation Tool you can use when touring facilities. This tool will help you keep track of which facility you like best. You should make a separate copy of the blank form for each facility you plan to visit.

chapter **6**

NURSING HOME EVALUATION TOOL

A s you visit nursing homes, use the following form for each place you visit. Don't expect every nursing home to score well on every question. The presence or absence of any of these items does not automatically mean a facility is good or bad. Each has its own strengths and weaknesses. Simply consider what is most important to the resident and you.

Record your observations for each question by circling a number from one to five. If a question is unimportant to you or doesn't apply to your loved one, leave the evaluation area for that question blank. Then total all numbers circled for each facility.

Your ratings will help you compare nursing homes and choose the best one for your situation. The facilities with the highest scores are those on which you should focus your final attention. However, you shouldn't rely solely on the numbers. Ask to speak to family members of other residents. Also, contact the local or state ombudsman for information about the nursing home and get a copy of the facility's state inspection report from the nursing home, the agency that licenses nursing homes, or the ombudsman.

NURSING HOME EVALUATION TOOL

Name of Nursing Home: _____

Date Visited: _____

RATING SCALE				
Unacceptable	Acceptable	Average	Above Average	Excellent
1	2	3	4	5

THE BUILDING AND ITS SURROUNDINGS:

What is your first impression of the facility?	1 2 3 4 5
What is the condition of the facility's exterior paint, gutters and trim?	1 2 3 4 5
Are the grounds pleasant and well-kept?	1 2 3 4 5
Do you like the view from residents' rooms and other windows?	1 2 3 4 5
Are there appropriate areas for physical therapy and occupational therapy?	1 2 3 4 5
Do chairs and other furniture seem sturdy and difficult to tip? Are they attractive and comfortable?	1 2 3 4 5
Do patient beds in double rooms have privacy curtains?	1 2 3 4 5
Are those curtains being used by staff to protect the privacy of patients receiving treatments or assistance?	1 2 3 4 5

Is an on-site barber or beauty salon available?	1 2 3 4 5
Is an on-site library available?	1 2 3 4 5
Is an on-site computer center with high speed internet access available?	1 2 3 4 5
Is an on-site gift shop available?	1 2 3 4 5
Is an on-site general store available?	1 2 3 4 5
Do meals appear appetizing and are they served promptly at the proper times?	1 2 3 4 5
Do residents who need help eating receive adequate assistance?	1 2 3 4 5
Is the dining area clean and pleasant?	1 2 3 4 5
Is there room at and between tables for both residents and aides for those who need assistance with meals?	1 2 3 4 5
What is the level and enthusiasm of resident participation in the activities?	1 2 3 4 5
Is there a well-ventilated indoor room for smokers?	1 2 3 4 5
Is there a covered / enclosed outdoor shelter for smokers?	1 2 3 4 5
Are non-smoking rules enforced, both indoors and outdoors, in all non-smoking areas?	1 2 3 4 5
What is your impression of general cleanliness throughout the facility?	1 2 3 4 5
What is your impression of the general cleanliness and grooming of residents?	1 2 3 4 5

Does the facility smell clean?	1 2 3 4 5
Is there enough space in resident rooms and common areas for the number of residents?	1 2 3 4 5
How noisy are hallways and common areas?	1 2 3 4 5
Are common areas such as lounges and activity rooms provided?	1 2 3 4 5
Are residents allowed to bring furniture and other personal items to decorate their rooms?	1 2 3 4 5
Do residents with Alzheimer's disease live in a separate Alzheimer's unit?	1 2 3 4 5
Does the facility provide a secure outdoor area?	1 2 3 4 5
Is there a secure area where a resident with Alzheimer's can safely wander on paths?	1 2 3 4 5

THE STAFF, POLICIES AND PRACTICES:

Does the administrator know residents by name and speak to them in a pleasant, friendly way?	1 2 3 4 5
Do staff and residents communicate with cheerful, respectful attitudes?	1 2 3 4 5
Do staff and administration seem to work well with each other in a spirit of cooperation?	1 2 3 4 5
Do residents get permanent assignment of staff?	1 2 3 4 5

Do nursing assistants participate in the resident's care planning process?	1 2 3 4 5
How good is the facility's record for employee retention?	1 2 3 4 5
Does a state ombudsman visit the facility on a regular basis?	1 2 3 4 5
How likely is an increase in private pay rates?	1 2 3 4 5
Are there any additional charges not included in the daily or monthly rate?	1 2 3 4 5

QUESTIONS TO ASK THE STAFF:

Are beds available?	1 2 3 4 5
What method is used in matching roommates?	1 2 3 4 5
What is a typical day like?	1 2 3 4 5
Can residents choose what time to go to bed and wake up?	1 2 3 4 5
Are meaningful activities available that are appropriate for residents?	1 2 3 4 5
Is there an activities schedule posted? Are residents engaged in activities?	1 2 3 4 5
Can residents continue to participate in interests like gardening or contact with pets?	1 2 3 4 5
Does the facility provide transportation for religious services and other activities?	1 2 3 4 5

Is a van or bus with wheelchair access available?	1 2 3 4 5
How are decisions about method and frequency of bathing made?	1 2 3 4 5
How do residents get their clothes laundered?	1 2 3 4 5
What happens when clothing or other items are missing?	1 2 3 4 5
Does the facility have a current license from the state?	1 2 3 4 5
Does the administrator have a current license from the state?	1 2 3 4 5
If Medicare and/or Medicaid coverage is needed, is the facility certified?	1 2 3 4 5
Does the facility have a formal quality assurance program?	1 2 3 4 5
Does the facility have an operating agreement with a nearby hospital for emergencies?	1 2 3 4 5
Is a physician available in an emergency?	1 2 3 4 5
Are personal physicians allowed?	1 2 3 4 5
How is regular medical attention assured?	1 2 3 4 5
How are patients and families involved in treatment plans?	1 2 3 4 5
Are specialty medical services available (e.g., dentists, podiatrists, optometrists)?	1 2 3 4 5
Does the facility report to the patient's personal physician on progress? To families?	1 2 3 4 5

What services are provided for terminally ill patients and their families?	1 2 3 4 5
Is a licensed nurse always available?	1 2 3 4 5
Does a pharmacist review patient drug regimens?	1 2 3 4 5
Are arrangement made for patients to worship or attend religious services?	1 2 3 4 5
Is physical therapy available under the direction of a licensed physical therapist?	1 2 3 4 5
Are services of an occupational therapist or speech pathologist available?	1 2 3 4 5
How are residents encouraged to participate in activities?	1 2 3 4 5
How are patient activity preferences respected?	1 2 3 4 5
Are both group and individual activities available?	1 2 3 4 5
Is a social worker available to assist residents and families?	1 2 3 4 5
Does a dietician plan menus for patients on special diets?	1 2 3 4 5
Are personal likes and dislikes taken into consideration in menu planning?	1 2 3 4 5
Are snacks available between meals?	1 2 3 4 5

Are the number of meals / snacks provided adequate?	1 2 3 4 5
Is the food preparation area separate from the dishwashing and garbage areas?	1 2 3 4 5
Is food which needs refrigeration put away promptly, and not left standing on counters?	1 2 3 4 5
Is there fresh water on bedside stands?	1 2 3 4 5
Are there hand rails in hallways and grab bars in bathrooms?	1 2 3 4 5
Are toilets convenient to bedrooms?	1 2 3 4 5
Is there a sink in each bathroom?	1 2 3 4 5
Are call bells near each toilet?	1 2 3 4 5
Are the hallways wide enough to accommodate passing wheelchairs?	1 2 3 4 5
Are the rooms large enough to allow a wheelchair to maneuver easily?	1 2 3 4 5
Is the temperature comfortable (remember many seniors prefer warmer environments)?	1 2 3 4 5
Does every patient room have a window?	1 2 3 4 5
Do all residents have closets and drawers for clothing?	1 2 3 4 5
Is the atmosphere generally friendly and welcoming?	1 2 3 4 5
If residents call out for help or use a call light, do they get prompt, appropriate responses?	1 2 3 4 5

Does each resident have the same nursing assistant(s) most of the time?	1 2 3 4 5
How does a resident with problems voice a complaint?	1 2 3 4 5
How are disputes, problems, or complaints with the quality of care resolved?	1 2 3 4 5
Are residents who are able to permitted to participate in care plan meetings?	1 2 3 4 5
Does the facility have an effective resident council?	1 2 3 4 5
Is an effective family council in place?	1 2 3 4 5
Can family/staff meetings be scheduled to discuss and work out any problems that may arise?	1 2 3 4 5

QUESTIONS TO ASK YOURSELF:

Do I feel comfortable coming here/leaving my loved one here?	1 2 3 4 5
How convenient is the facility's location to me and other family members who may want to visit the resident?	1 2 3 4 5
Are there areas other than the resident's room where family members can visit?	1 2 3 4 5
Does the facility have safe, well-lighted, convenient parking?	1 2 3 4 5
Are hotels/motels nearby for out-of-town family members?	1 2 3 4 5

Are there restaurants nearby suitable for taking the resident out for a meals with family members?	1 2 3 4 5
How convenient will care planning conferences be for interested family members?	1 2 3 4 5
Is the facility convenient for the patient's personal physician?	1 2 3 4 5

Total Score: _____

chapter 7

HOW TO PAY FOR THE NURSING HOME

One of greatest concerns people have about nursing home care is how to pay for it. There are basically four ways to pay for the cost of the care provided by a nursing home:

Private Pay. This is the method many people must use at first. It means paying for the cost of a nursing home out of your own pocket. Unfortunately, with nursing home bills of more than $12,000 per month at some facilities, few people can afford to pay on their own for a long-term stay in a nursing home. Even those who can afford to do so often desire to explore other options — options that allow them to retain some or all of their assets for other important needs, while still permitting them to pay for nursing home care.

Long-Term Care Insurance. If you have long-term care insurance coverage, this could help pay the costs of needed home care or nursing home care. Unfortunately, only about ten percent of the population carry long-term care insurance, so most people facing a nursing home stay do not have this type of coverage in place. Many people who would like to purchase this type of coverage find that they can not afford it. How to purchase the best long-term care policy is a complicated subject that is well-worth exploring if you are in your 50s or 60s

Long-Term Care Insurance should be given serious consideration if it is affordable for you, especially in view of the new federally-mandated Long-Term Care Partnership, which allows you to use long-term care insurance as a type of Medicaid Asset Protection.

and still healthy. It should be given serious consideration if it is affordable for you, especially in view of the new federally-mandated "Long-Term Care Partnership," which allows you to use long-term care insurance as a type of Medicaid Asset Protection – to protect an amount of assets equivalent to the premium paid for the insurance. If you are thinking about purchasing a long-term care insurance policy, an experienced elder law attorney can assist you in finding the best policy by helping you compare and contrast the numerous types of policies available and the different types and levels of coverage offered, as well as the independent ratings and financial stability of the insurance company providing the coverage. You should also discuss with an elder law attorney some of the uses of, and alternatives to, long-term care insurance, so that you have a better understanding of the cost versus benefit of such coverage. You will find additional information about Long-Term Care Insurance starting on page 38.

Department of Veterans Affairs. The Department of Veterans Affairs (VA) primarily pays for long-term care through the Veterans "Aid and Attendance" Special Pension Benefit payments. In some parts of the country, there are also nursing homes that are run by the Department of Veterans Affairs. You will find additional information about the Veterans "Aid and Attendance" Special Pension starting on page 46.

Medicaid. This is a combined federally-funded and state-funded benefit program, administered by each state, that can pay for the cost of a nursing home if certain asset and income tests are met. According to AARP, about 70 percent of nursing home residents are supported, at least in part, by Medicaid. Medicaid qualification and eligibility will be discussed in greater detail starting on page 52.

A WORD ABOUT MEDICARE

You will notice that Medicare is NOT listed among the sources of funds used to pay for long-term care in a nursing home. This is because Medicare does not pay a penny for long-term care, ever.

Medicare is the national health insurance program primarily for people 65 years of age and older, those under age 65 who have been disabled for at least 24 months, and people with kidney failure. Medicare may provide some coverage for short-term (up to 100 days) rehabilitation in a nursing facility, provided you continue to get better from the rehabilitation, but you must meet certain strict qualification rules, which will be discussed in greater detail starting on page 36.

chapter 8

WHAT DOES MEDICARE COVER?

M ost people have a great deal of confusion between *Medicare* and *Medicaid.*

Medicare is a federally-funded and federally-administered health insurance program, primarily designed for individuals over age 65. Medicare does not cover long-term care under any circumstances.

If you are enrolled in a traditional Medicare plan, and you've been in the hospital at least three days, and you are admitted directly from the hospital into a rehab facility (which are typically skilled nursing facilities) for short-term rehabilitation (i.e., therapy and treatment designed to make you better), then Medicare should pay the full cost of this short-term rehab stay for the first 20 days, and may continue to pay part of the cost of the short-term rehab stay for the next 80 days — with a per day deductible that you must pay privately (although there are Medicare

> *It is important to understand that Medicare does not pay one penny for long-term care.*

supplement insurance policies that sometimes cover that deductible). There is also a Medicare Managed Care Plan, for which the 3-day hospital stay may not be required, and for which the deductible for days 21 through 100 is waived, provided certain strict qualifying rules are met. But whether the plan is traditional Medicare or Medicare Managed Care (MMC), the nursing home resident must be receiving daily rehabilitative care and must be improving.   Medicare **does not pay** for long-term care, *i.e.*, for custodial nursing home stays or in-home care.

In a best case scenario, traditional Medicare or MMC will provide some coverage for the hospital stay and rehabilitation of up to 100 days for each "spell of illness" (although in our experience coverage usually falls far short of the 100-day maximum). If you recover sufficiently that you do not require a Medicare-covered care benefit for 60 consecutive days, you may be eligible for another benefit period, *i.e.*, another 100 days of Medicare coverage, but the illness or disorder must not be a chronic degenerative condition from which you will not recover.

What happens if you've used up the 100 days of coverage and still need more rehabilitation, or if you need to move into long-term nursing home care? You're back to one of the alternatives outlined above: long-term care insurance, paying the bills with your own assets, or qualifying for Medicaid.

chapter **9**

LONG-TERM CARE INSURANCE

L ong-term care insurance, for some people, can be a good way to provide for future long-term care needs. If you have long-term care insurance coverage, this could help pay the costs of needed nursing home care. Unfortunately, only about ten percent of the population carry long-term care insurance, so most people facing a nursing home stay do not have this type of coverage in place. Many people who would like to purchase this type of coverage find that they can not afford it.

However, this type of insurance coverage is worth exploring if you are under age 65 and still healthy, especially in view of the federally-mandated "Long-Term Care Partnership," which allows you to use special long-term care insurance for Medicaid Asset Protection – to protect an amount of assets equivalent to the total amount of insurance coverage you purchase.

If you are thinking about purchasing a long-term care insurance policy, an experienced, independent insurance agent who specializes in long-term care insurance can assist you in finding the best policy by helping you compare and contrast the numerous types of policies available and the different types and levels of coverage offered, as well as the independent ratings and financial stability of the insurance company providing the coverage.

Elder law attorneys are uniquely qualified to assess and address all of the issues that a client needing long-term care will face.

Consideration should be given to purchasing a long-term care insurance policy that covers home care only, as nursing home care can be paid for with Medicaid through proper Medicaid Asset Protection discussed later starting on page 52.

Additionally, you should discuss with a qualified elder law attorney some of the alternatives to long-term care insurance, so that you have a better understanding of the cost versus benefit of such coverage. Elder law attorneys are uniquely qualified to assess and address **all** of the issues that a client needing long-term care will face. Most insurance agents do not have a complete understanding of nursing home laws and Medicaid laws, and are usually not able to adequately address all of the issues surrounding long-term care.

WHAT ELDER LAW ISSUES MUST BE CONSIDERED WHEN PURCHASING LONG-TERM CARE INSURANCE?

When shopping for a long-term care insurance policy, it is crucial to consider carefully the entire financial situation of both spouses and to consider the possible alternative of not purchasing long-term care insurance. Failure to do so can result in purchasing too little coverage, too much coverage, or coverage for the wrong spouse, each of which can actually be worse than purchasing no coverage at all.

EXAMPLE OF PURCHASING TOO LITTLE COVERAGE

Consider Joe and Linda, a married couple facing Joe's nursing home costs of $8,500 per month. Joe has $4,000 in monthly retirement income, as well as a long-term care insurance policy with a monthly benefit of $4,500 (based on a daily benefit of $150). Linda's only income is Social Security of $700 per month. At first glance, the couple seems better off with the long-term care policy; they have an extra $4,500 per month, without which they could not afford the nursing home. With the insurance, Joe has exactly enough income to pay the private rate of the nursing home. Unfortunately, Linda's monthly expenses, even with Joe in the nursing home, are approximately $2,200 per month, and Joe is not eligible for Medicaid assistance because his income (including the long-term care insurance benefit) is sufficient to pay the private nursing home bill.

In this example, Joe's long-term care insurance policy does not provide enough of a benefit to allow Linda to have sufficient income to meet her needs. If Joe's long-term care insurance policy had provided a $6,000 monthly benefit ($200 per day instead of $150), then Joe would have income of $10,000 per month and $1,500 of Joe's retirement income would be available for Linda's monthly expenses. Joe's extra $1,500 per month plus Linda's own $700 per month would be just enough income for Linda to live on. Joe and Linda could have fully financed Joe's long-term care needs and ensured that Linda would have enough funds to meet her monthly expenses.

If Joe and Linda had recognized this shortfall and decided to not purchase the long-term care insurance, or if they could not afford the increased premiums for the increased monthly benefit, they could instead use Medicaid assistance to help pay for Joe's nursing home costs. Most of Joe's $4,000 per month of income would normally be required to pay the nursing home expenses; Linda would keep her $700 per month. However, because Linda's income is so low, the Medicaid rules would allow Linda to receive part of Joe's income to help her with her monthly living expenses. Linda could receive a monthly maintenance needs allowance of up to $2,841[3] (including her income) which includes allowances for housing and utilities. Therefore, in this case, Joe and Linda would have the nursing home costs paid, and Linda would have up to $2,841 monthly for her support.

The bottom line? Either buy enough long-term care insurance coverage or don't buy any. It doesn't make sense to pay insurance premiums and then be bankrupted by nursing home fees anyway because of insufficient coverage. And if you do buy coverage, be

---

[3]This is the maximum monthly maintenance needs allowance as of May, 2012.

sure to get adequate inflation coverage. As with other medical expenses, the inflation rate in nursing home fees is currently quite high. In 10 years, the cost of the nursing homes, at the current rate of inflation, will be about twice what it is today.

WHICH SPOUSE SHOULD GET COVERAGE?

Often a married couple will be able to afford coverage for only one spouse. *Statistics alone* would dictate that the wife should purchase the policy, as women tend to live longer than men are therefore more likely than men to end up in a nursing home for a long period of time. However, this is often the wrong answer! For a couple where the husband's retirement income is much higher than the wife's retirement income, it is actually much more important to purchase coverage for the husband. As just explained, if the husband enters the nursing without adequate long-term care coverage, the wife may wind up destitute or without sufficient income to live on.

The other half of the story is what happens if the wife goes into the nursing home first. Using the same fact scenario, let's now assume that Linda enters the nursing home first and does not have long-term care

> *For a couple where the husband's retirement income is much higher than the wife's retirement income, it is actually much more beneficial to purchase long-term care insurance for the husband.*

coverage. Is there any problem? No, not at all, because we can get Linda's nursing home paid for almost entirely through Medicaid assistance. Linda's $700 monthly income would have to go to the nursing home, but Medicaid will pay the rest. Joe will be able to keep 100% of his retirement income and, with proper Medicaid Asset Protection Planning, will be able to keep all of his assets.

HOW MUCH COVERAGE DO I NEED?

I don't recommend anyone purchasing more than five years of long-term care insurance coverage. For one reason, the average nursing home stay is only approximately 3 years. Secondly, after moving to a nursing home, your family can commence the process of Medicaid Asset Protection, which is the primary focus of my practice as and Elder Law attorney. Using Medicaid Asset Protection, we can have you transfer your assets into a special type of asset protection trust. After five years have passed, if you are still alive, you'll be able to qualify for Medicaid to pay your nursing home costs (provided the assets remaining in your name do not exceed Medicaid's limits). Using this strategy, you'll only need long-term care coverage only for five years before Medicaid coverage commences, so there's no need to purchase more than five years of long-term care coverage.

HOW DO I KNOW IF I CAN AFFORD LTC INSURANCE?

You should generally only purchase long-term care insurance if you can pay the premiums out of your disposable income, i.e, if the premiums are affordable using income that you would otherwise add to your savings.

HOW CAN I REDUCE MY PREMIUM?

There are five ways to reduce the cost of LTC Insurance. First, request a one-hundred day elimination period since Medicare may pay some or all of the first hundred days (to the extent skilled nursing care is required). Second, the daily benefit purchased can be reduced by income from pensions and Social Security, to the extent these items may not be needed by a spouse. Third, the benefit period should be limited to five years since this will encompass the majority of claims and the Medicaid look-back period for transfers does not exceed that period. Fourth, work with an independent agent who can provide at least three premium quotes. Some clients end up paying too much due to transactions with captive agents. Fifth, the cost of the insurance may be reduced forty to fifty percent by choosing a home-care only policy — an especially attractive option for clients who either cannot afford complete protection, are willing to rely on Medicaid Planning for Nursing Home protection, or for those over age seventy where the expense tends to be prohibitive.

WHEN IS THE BEST TIME TO PURCHASE COVERAGE?

If you decide that long term care insurance is the right decision to protect your assets and your family's financial future, the best time to buy it is now, because the older you get, the more expensive the policy becomes in the long run. By buying now:

- You avoid the risk of needing care you will have to pay for yourself.

- You avoid the risk of developing a condition that would make you uninsurable later.

- You pay lower premiums now, rather than paying higher premiums later.

  The sample table below shows the cost for a 44-year old male of waiting and buying later, assuming that premiums do not change and the applicant remains insurable. The Daily Benefit is increased 5% for each year of waiting, to cover the increased cost of care over time.

Age at Purchase	Daily Benefit	Premium	Premiums Paid to Age 90	Cost of Waiting
44	$200	$1,598	$73,508	$0
46	$221	$1,893	$83,292	$9,784
48	$243	$2,232	$93,730	$20,222
50	$268	$2,643	$105,707	$32,199
52	$295	$3,039	$115,487	$41,979
54	$326	$3,489	$125,607	$52,099

WHAT BENEFITS AND RIDERS ARE MOST IMPORTANT?

The most important benefits are inflation protection, as mentioned above, and a stay-at-home option. Some long-term care insurance policies limit the amount of home care coverage. For example, a policy may pay $200 per day for nursing home care, but only $150 per day for home care; this is an example of a 75% home care benefit. Given that almost everyone needing long-term care prefers to remain in his or her own home for as long as possible, a 100% home care benefit is an essential option.

TAX DEDUCTIBILITY OF LONG-TERM CARE INSURANCE PREMIUMS

Federal Income Tax: Under the Health Insurance Portability and Accountability Act ("HIPAA"), "qualified" long-term care insurance policies receive special tax treatment. To be "qualified," policies must adhere to regulations established by the National Association of Insurance Commissioners:

- The policy must offer the consumer the options of "inflation" and "nonforfeiture" protection, although the consumer can choose not to purchase these features.

- The policies must also offer both activities of daily living ("ADL") and cognitive impairment triggers, but may not offer a medical necessity trigger. "Triggers" are conditions that must be present for a policy to be activated.

- Premiums for "qualified" long-term care policies will be treated as a medical expense and will be deductible from Federal Income Tax to the extent that they, along with other unreimbursed medical expenses (including "Medigap" insurance premiums) exceed 7.5 percent of the insured's adjusted gross income. But the deductibility of premiums is limited by the age of the taxpayer at the end of the year.

State Income Tax: Many states have programs allowing a deduction from state income taxes.

MIGHT THE LTC INSURANCE COMPANY GO OUT OF BUSINESS?

Yes. Several long-term care insurance companies have gone bankrupt. Of course it's important to deal with top-rated companies, but even some top-rated companies have gotten out of the long-term care insurance business in recent years, so buying these policies definitely involves some degree of risk.

chapter 10

VETERANS AID & ATTENDANCE

T he Department of Veteran Affairs pays for long-term care primarily through its "Aid and Attendance" payments, which is actually a Special Pension with add-on for Aid & Attendance.

ELIGIBILITY REQUIREMENTS

To be an eligible veteran, you must have served 90 days active duty, at least one day during a period of war, and must have not been dishonorably discharged. If you entered active duty after September 7, 1980, generally you must have served at least 24 months or the full period for which called or ordered to active duty and at least 1 day was during a war time period (though there are exceptions to this rule). For a Veteran's surviving spouse to be eligible, the surviving

PERIODS OF WARTIME:

World War II: December 7, 1941 through December 31, 1946

Korean Conflict: June 27, 1950 through January 31, 1955

Vietnam Era: August 5, 1964 through May 7, 1975; for veterans who served "in country" before August 5, 1964, February 28, 1961 through May 7, 1975

Current Era: August 2, 1990 through a date to be set by law or

spouse must have been married for at least one year to the veteran at the time of death or had children with the veteran. Divorce or remarriage excludes qualification.

MEDICAL QUALIFICATION

Once you are determined to be an eligible veteran, the next question is whether you are medically qualified. If you are age 65 and older, there is no requirement to prove disability. However, you or spouse must be in need of regular aid and attendance due to:

- inability to dress or undress yourself, or to keep yourself ordinarily clean and presentable;

- frequent need of adjustment of any special prosthetic or orthopedic appliances which by reason of the particular disability cannot be done without aid (this will not include the adjustment of appliances which normal persons would be unable to adjust without aid, such as supports, belts, lacing at the back etc.);

- inability to feed yourself through loss of coordination of upper extremities or through extreme weakness;

- inability to attend to the wants of nature; or

- incapacity, physical or mental, which requires care or assistance on a regular basis to protect you from hazards or dangers incident to your daily environment.

Not all of the disabling conditions in the list above are required to exist. It is only necessary that the evidence establish that you or your spouse needs "regular" (scheduled and ongoing) aid and attendance from someone else, not that there be a 24-hour need.

If you are not at least 65 years of age or older, then you must be permanently and totally disabled (not due to your own willful misconduct), or a patient in a nursing home, or receiving Social Security Disability benefits.

Determinations of a need for the aid and attendance is based on medical reports and findings by private physicians or from hospital facilities. Authorization of aid and attendance is automatic if evidence establishes the claimant is a patient in a nursing home or that the claimant is blind or nearly blind or having severe visual problems.

NET WORTH QUALIFICATION

There is no set limit on how much net worth a Veteran and his or her dependents can have to qualify financially for the Aid and Attendance benefit. According to the Department of Veteran Affairs, "net worth cannot be excessive." Unfortunately, the VA does not define "excessive," but rather makes the vague and sweeping statement that the decision as to whether a Veteran's net worth is "excessive" depends on the facts of each individual case. The VA says it looks at all of the claimants's assets and determines "if a Veteran's assets are of a sufficient amount that the claimant could live off these assets for a reasonable period of time."

In my practice, I have found that a reasonable amount of money for a Veteran to retain to be ensured of receiving this benefit is approximately $10,000. For Veterans with more money than this, there are numerous asset protection strategies that can we can employ to you and your family legally and ethically protect the excess assets.

INCOME QUALIFICATION

Many Veterans are mistakenly led to believe that Aid and Attendance is only for Veterans with very low income. The website

> *Many Veterans are mistakenly led to believe that Aid and Attendance is only for Veterans with very low income.*

of the Department of Veterans Affairs says that this program is for "wartime Veterans who have limited or no income." If you speak to a Veterans Service Representative in a regional VA office and ask them about the Veterans Aid and Attendance benefit, they will ask for your household income. When you tell them your household income, they will compare it to a chart and most often tell you that you earn too much income to receive the benefit. While the information they provide may be technically accurate, what they typically don't explain is the "income" for VA purposes (sometimes called IVAP or "adjusted income") is actually your household income **minus** certain recurring, unreimbursed medical and long-term care expenses. These allowable, annualized medical expenses are such things as health insurance premiums, home health care expenses, the cost of paying a family member or other person to provide care, the cost of adult day care, the cost of an assisted living facility, or the cost of a nursing home.

To be able to receive the Veterans Pension with Aid and Attendance benefit, the veteran household cannot have adjusted income (i.e., household income minus unreimbursed medical expenses) exceeding the Maximum Allowable Pension Rate -- MAPR -- for that veteran's Pension income category. If the adjusted income exceeds MAPR, there is no benefit. If adjusted income is less than the MAPR, the veteran receives a Pension income that is equal to the difference between MAPR and the household income adjusted for unreimbursed medical expenses. The Pension income is calculated based on 12 months of future household income, but paid monthly.

MAXIMUM BENEFIT

As of 2012, the maximum possible benefit (i.e., the maximum MAPR) for the Aid and Attendance Benefit is as follows:

• Single Veteran - $20,447 per year (~$1,704/month)
• Married Veteran - $24,239 per year (~$2,020/month)
• Surviving Spouse - $13,138 per year (~$1,095/month)
• Married Vets both w/need - $31,578 per year (~$2,631/ month)

How is the Benefit Calculated?

The monthly award is based on VA totaling 12 months of estimated future income and subtracting from that 12 months of estimated future, recurring and predictable medical expenses. Allowable medical expenses are reduced by a deductible to produce an adjusted medical expense which in turn is subtracted from the estimated 12 months of future income.

The net income derived from subtracting adjusted medical expenses from income is called "countable" income or IVAP (Income for Veterans Affairs Purposes). This countable income is then subtracted from the Maximum Allowable Pension Rate -- MAPR -- and that result is divided by 12 to determine the monthly income Pension award. Medical expenses must exceed income by 5% for the maximum benefit. This award is paid in addition to the family income that already exists.

Examples of Benefit Calculations

Assume two veterans living in the same assisted living facility, both having the same supplemental health insurance, one with retirement income of $4,880 per month and the other with retirement income of $4,642.70 per month.

Here's the calculation of the Countable Unreimbursed Monthly Medical Expenses for both veterans:

Assisted Living Facility	$4,500.00
Plus Medicare Part B	$99.90
Plus Medicare Supplemental Insurance	$128.00
Equals Total Monthly Unreimbursed Medical Expenses	$4,727.90
Minus 5% of Maximum Benefit ($1,704)	$-85.20
Equals Countable Unreimbursed Monthly Medical Expenses	$4,642.70

Here's the calculation of the IVAP and the total aid & attendance benefit per month for the first veteran:

Total Monthly Income	$ 4,880.00
Less Countable Unreimbursed Medical Expenses	$ -4,642.70
Equals IVAP	$ 237.30

Maximum Aid & Attendance Benefit	$ 1,704.00
Less IVAP	$ -237.30
Equals Total Aid & Attendance Benefit per Month	$ 1,466.70

Here's the calculation of the IVAP and the total aid & attendance benefit per month for the second veteran:

Total Monthly Income	$ 4,642.70
Less Countable Unreimbursed Medical Expenses	$ -4,642.70
Equals IVAP	$ 0.00

Maximum Aid & Attendance Benefit	$ 1,704.00
Less IVAP	$ 0.00
Equals Total Aid & Attendance Benefit per Month	$ 1,704.00

chapter **11**

MEDICAID BASICS

A society will be judged on how it treats those in the dawn of life, those in the twilight of life, and those in the shadow of life.

- Hubert Humphrey

There are many different types of Medicaid, but the Medicaid that will be discussed in this book is the governmental benefits program that pays for Americans who need custodial long-term care, typically provided in nursing homes. Medicaid is funded by federal and state taxes and administered by each state. While the rules for eligibility vary from state to state, the primary benefit of Medicaid is that it will pay for long-term care in a nursing home once an individual has qualified. As mentioned previously, according to AARP about 70 percent of nursing home residents are supported, at least in part, by Medicaid. Most importantly, long-term care paid for by the Medicaid program is legally required to be of the same quality as that of a private pay patient.

The current societal crisis posed by the increasing need for long- term care is a relatively new one. Prior to the advent of nursing homes in the 1950s, those seniors who lived into old age were typically cared for in the homes of their children.

> *Healthier lifestyles and advances in modern medicine have been causing Americans to live longer and longer. Unfortunately, this increased life expectancy means that Americans are often out-living their ability to care for themselves.*

Life expectancy was such that most people died before the advent of chronic diseases such as Alzheimer's. Healthier lifestyles and advances in modern medicine have been causing Americans to live longer and longer. Unfortunately, this increased life expectancy means that Americans are often out-living their ability to care for themselves.

Many Americans falsely believe that Medicare will provide chronic/custodial care for themselves and their parents. These people are shocked when they learn the truth — that Medicaid, not Medicare, is the only governmental benefit available to pay for long-term care.

Medicaid, created in 1965 under President Lyndon Johnson, has effectively become the long-term care insurance of the middle class because of the simple fact that very few people can afford to pay the national average of $87,235 per year for a private room or even the $78,110 per year for a semi-private room.[4] As the primary source of nursing home funding in the United States, Medicaid is one of the Federal Government's three "social contracts" with America — the other two being Social Security (which provides retirement income for older Americans), and Medicare (which provides health coverage).

In 2005 Senator Rockefeller, then the ranking member of the Senate Finance Committee's Subcommittee on Health Care, in marking the 40th anniversary of the Medicaid program, stated that

> "President Johnson's noble concept was not just a Democratic ideal; it had been an inspiration shared throughout the early part of the century by legislators and presidents from both parties. And since the signing of the landmark legislation, administrations - both Republican and Democratic - have fought to preserve the Medicaid mission of providing healthcare for the nation's most vulnerable citizens.
>
> "Sadly, in the past few years, we have seen a misguided,

---

[4] "The MetLife Market Survey of Nursing Home, Assisted Living Costs, Adult Day Services, and Home Care Costs." October 2011.
http://www.metlife.com/mmi/research/2011-market-survey-long-term-care-costs.html

darker view of Medicaid emerge - one that loses sight of its original goal and underlying moral framework. Medicaid has become a scapegoat for the larger ills facing our entire healthcare system. But Medicaid isn't the problem. . . . Taking care of our most vulnerable people is a moral obligation.

"Our representative democracy has a responsibility to do for the future what we have repeatedly done in the past: protect, preserve, and strengthen Medicaid."

APPLYING FOR MEDICAID - WHY YOU NEED HELP

Sixteen years after the creation of Medicaid, the United States Supreme Court called the Medicaid laws "an aggravated assault on the English language, resistant to attempts to understand it." *Schweiker v. Gray Panthers*, 453 U.S. 34, 43 (1981). Thirteen years later, the United States Court of Appeals for the Fourth Circuit called the Medicaid Act one of the "most completely impenetrable texts within human experience" and "dense reading of the most tortuous kind." *Rehabilitation Ass'n of Va. v. Kozlowski*, 42 F.3d 1444, 1450 (4th Cir. 1994). Since then, it has only gotten worse.

Congress enacted the Deficit Reduction Act of 2005 on June 23, 2006, retroactive to February 8, 2006, the date of enactment, which rewrote a huge portion of the Medicaid law.

> *The United States Supreme Court called the Medicaid laws "an aggravated assault on the English language, resistant to attempts to understand it."*

The actual Medicaid application process differs from state to state, but it typically involves filling out a lengthy and detailed application and also submitting appropriate verifications of income, assets, transfers, identity, and citizenship.

Due to tremendous complexity of the Medicaid laws, the Medicaid application process is also extremely complicated, and many persons who file for Medicaid without professional assistance will wind up with the application being rejected for a variety of reasons. Rejection often occurs due to financial issues — either excess resources, excess income, or improperly-timed gifts or transfers. Rejection in many cases is due to missing or incomplete information or verifications. Applications are also sometimes improperly rejected by an eligibility worker (most of whom are underpaid and overworked) who has not had the time to carefully and thoroughly review the application and verifications, or who has improperly applied the legal or financial requirements for eligibility.

The Fourth Circuit has called the Medicaid Act one of the "most completely impenetrable texts within human experience" and "dense reading of the most tortuous kind."

Worse yet, an application that is filed at the wrong time can result not only in rejection, but in the imposition of significant penalties against the applicant that could have been avoided by a more timely filing. For these and many other reasons, an experienced elder law attorney should always be hired to represent the applicant through the entire Medicaid process — including planning for eligibility (including, if necessary, Medicaid Asset Protection), preparing and filing the application, working with the local eligibility department during the application and verification process, filing an appeal when necessary, and representing the applicant in connection with any required hearings and appeals.

WHO CAN GET MEDICAID?

Almost anyone can get Medicaid. Medicaid is not a program for poor people. It is a program for anyone who can meet the eligibility criteria. Those criteria will be explained in detail in the next several sections.

OVERVIEW OF MEDICAID ELIGIBILITY CRITERIA

There are four separate but overlapping eligibility criteria for Medicaid, each of which is discussed below in detail:

- Medical Eligibility;

- Resource Eligibility;

- Income Eligibility; and

- Transfer Eligibility.

MEDICAL ELIGIBILITY

To be eligible for Medicaid long-term care assistance in most states, you must generally be "medically needy" – meaning in need of a nursing home level of care, though some states have expanded Medicaid to cover the assisted living level of care. Determination of eligibility for long-term medical care is typically based on a comprehensive needs assessment, which must demonstrate that the proposed Medicaid recipient requires nursing facility services. This individual may have unstable medical, behavioral and/or cognitive conditions, one or more of which may require ongoing nursing assessment, intervention, and/or referrals to other disciplines for evaluations and appropriate treatment. Often adult nursing facility residents have severe cognitive impairments and related problems with memory deficits and problem-solving. These impairments and deficits severely compromise personal safety and, therefore, require a structured, therapeutic environment. Most nursing facility residents are also dependent on others in several Activities of Daily Living (walking; transferring; feeding; dressing; bathing; and toileting).

RESOURCE ELIGIBILITY

In every state, an individual applicant for Medicaid long-term care assistance may have no more than a small amount in "countable resources" in his or her name in order to be "resource eligible" for Medicaid. For example, in Virginia, this Individual Resource Allowance is $2,000. A married couple both applying for Medicaid long-term care assistance may have no more than $3,000 total Resources Allowance in their names in order to be resource eligible for Medicaid.

EXEMPT ASSETS AND COUNTABLE ASSETS

To qualify for Medicaid, applicants must pass some very strict tests on the type and amount of assets they can keep. To understand how Medicaid works, one first needs to learn to differentiate what are known as "exempt assets" from "countable" assets. Exempt assets are those that Medicaid does not take into account. In most states, that includes:

- The applicant's principal residence so long as the equity is below the Home Equity Cap, which is currently $525,000 in most states, but as high as $750,000 or more in some states, and is indexed for inflation. However, in some states, such as Virginia, after the nursing

> *In every state, an individual applicant for Medicaid long-term care assistance may have no more than a small amount in "countable resources" in his or her name in order to be "resource eligible" for Medicaid.*

home resident has been in the nursing home for a period of time (*e.g.* six months in Virginia), the resident's home will become a countable resource unless the resident's spouse or other dependent relatives live in the home. When the home is an exempt resource, that means the Medicaid applicant can keep the home and still qualify for Medicaid. But it also means that the home will be part of the Medicaid recipient's estate at death and that the state can therefore exercise Estate Recovery (see page 59) against the home after death, thereby recovering from the sales proceeds of the home some or all of what Medicaid paid during the lifetime of the Medicaid recipient.

- Personal possessions, such as clothing, furniture, and jewelry.

- One motor vehicle, without regard to value.

- Certain property used in a trade or business.

- Certain prepaid burial arrangements.

- Term life insurance policies with no cash value.

- A life estate in real estate (however, the transfer rules on life estates are very complicated and must be carefully observed). Also, in some states, retention of a life estate means that the actuarial value of the life estate immediately prior to death will be considered to part of the Medicaid recipient's estate at death and that the state can therefore exercise Estate Recovery (see page 59) against the home after death, thereby recovering from the sales proceeds of the home some or all of what Medicaid paid during the lifetime of the Medicaid recipient.

- Certain Special Needs Trusts; and

- Certain assets that are considered inaccessible for one reason or another.

All other assets are generally "countable" assets, technically called "resources." Basically all money and property, and any item that can be valued and turned into cash, is a countable asset. This generally includes:

- Cash, savings and checking accounts, credit union share and draft accounts;

- Certificates of deposit;

- Individual Retirement Accounts (IRAs), Keogh plans, 401(k) and 403(b) accounts (though some states exempt retirement accounts if they are in some sort of "payout" status, even though they have a cash value);

- Nursing home accounts;

- Prepaid funeral contracts that can be canceled;

> *Most people mistakenly think that Medicaid is only for people with very low income. The actual rule for income is that a Medicaid applicant can qualify so long as his gross income is less than the private pay cost of the nursing home care he is receiving.*

- Certain trusts (depending on the terms of the trust);

- Real estate other than the primary residence;

- Any additional motor vehicles;

- Boats or recreational vehicles;

- Stocks, bonds, or mutual funds; and

- Land contracts or mortgages held on real estate.

ESTATE RECOVERY RULES

Under federal regulations and state laws, the Medicaid agency of every state may make a claim against a deceased Medicaid recipient's estate when the recipient was age 55 or over. The recovery can include any Medicaid payments made on his/her behalf. This claim can be waived if there are surviving dependents. One of the goals of Medicaid Asset Protection, discussed starting on page 66, is to prevent Estate Recovery.

INCOME ELIGIBILITY FOR MEDICAID

Most people mistakenly think that Medicaid is only for people with very low income. The actual rule for income is that a Medicaid applicant can qualify so long as his gross income is less than the private pay cost of the nursing home care he is receiving. A Medicaid recipient must pay all of his income, less certain deductions, to the nursing home. The deductions include a small monthly personal needs allowance which ranges from around $40 per month to $100 per month depending on the state, a deduction for certain uncovered medical expenses (such as medical insurance premiums) and, in the case of a married applicant, an allowance (called the Community Spouse Resource Allowance) the nursing home spouse may possibly be able to pay to the spouse that continues to live at home. See page 62 for more information about the Community Spouse Resource Allowance.

Some states are "medically needy" states and some states are "income cap" states. In "income cap" states, a Medicaid applicant must have income lower than a specified "cap." However, in those states a special trust, called a *Miller Trust* (also called a *Qualifying Income Trust*, a *Qualified Income Trust,* and *Income Cap Trust* or and *Income Assignment Trust*) is needed if the Medicaid applicant's income is above a certain level. The way the Miller Trust works is that after the trust is created, the patient assigns his or her right to receive social security and pension to the trust. In the eyes of the state Medicaid agency, if the Miller Trust is receiving income, the patient is not receiving that income, and thus the excess income "problem" is solved.

THE LOOKBACK PERIOD AND THE TRANSFER RULES

The Lookback Period for Medicaid is 5 years from the date of application. This means that when you file an application for Medicaid, you are asked whether you made any gifts (including charitable donations) or other uncompensated transfers during the

5 years prior to applying for Medicaid. Uncompensated transfers include things such as gambling losses and paying money for someone else's benefit, such as paying for a child's wedding or putting money into a fund for a grandchild's education.

UNCOMPENSATED TRANSFERS AND PENALTY PERIODS

Transfer Penalty. An uncompensated transfer of assets results in a period of ineligibility for Medicaid, typically called a "penalty period." The penalty period begins when (a) the person would be receiving an institutional level of care, (b) an application has been filed, and (c) a person is not in any other period of ineligibility. For most people this means at the time an application is filed and they are receiving care. It is important to understand that the transfer penalty period can be longer than 5 years. Some examples of how the penalty period is calculated are shown in below:

When you file an application for Medicaid, you are asked whether you made any gifts (including charitable donations) or other uncompensated transfers during the 5 years prior to applying for Medicaid.

Hypothetical State Penalty Divisor	=	$8,000

Amount Transferred	÷ 8000	=	Penalty Period	
$100,000.00	÷ 8000	=	12.5	Months
$150,000.00	÷ 8000	=	18.8	Months
$250,000.00	÷ 8000	=	31.3	Months
$500,000.00	÷ 8000	=	62.5	Months

PROTECTIONS FOR THE COMMUNITY SPOUSE

Federal law provides some basic built-in protection for married couples. This law recognizes that it is not fair to completely impoverish both spouses when only one spouse needs to qualify for Medicaid nursing home care.

Community Spouse Resource Allowance (CSRA): All countable assets owned by a married couple as of the "snapshot date" (the first day of the first month that the Medicaid applicant enters the nursing home or becomes "institutionalized," meaning a resident of a hospital and/or nursing home for more than 30 continuous days), regardless of whether titled jointly or in the name of just one spouse, are divided into equal halves. One-half of the countable assets (subject to a current maximum under Federal Law of $113,640 and minimum of $22,728[5]), is then allocated to the Community Spouse. This amount that is allocated to the community spouse is called the "Community Spouse Resource Allowance" or CSRA (sometimes called the Protected Resource Amount or PRA). The remaining assets are allocated to the nursing home spouse, and

---

[5] These amounts are as of 2012, and are subject to change annually – for updated numbers, see the author's website at
http://www.farrlawfirm.com/keyelderlawnumbers.htm. Some states are more generous and have a higher minimum CSRA, and some always allow the Community Spouse to retain the maximum CSRA, even if it is more than half of the snapshot amount.

must be reduced until only the Individual Resource Allowance remains, at which time the nursing home spouse will qualify for Medicaid. The examples below assume a state with a $2,000 Individual Resource Allowance.

- **Example 1:** John and Mary have $100,000 in combined resources just prior to the date John enters the nursing home. John will be eligible for Medicaid once the couple's combined assets have been reduced to $52,000 ($2,000 Individual Resource Allowance for John plus $50,000 for Mary as her Community Spouse Resource Allowance).

- **Example 2**: Bill and Nancy have $200,000 in combined resources just prior to the date Nancy enters the nursing home. Nancy will be eligible for Medicaid once the couple's combined assets have been reduced to $102,000 ($2,000 Individual Resource Allowance for Nancy plus $100,000 for Bill as his Community Spouse Resource Allowance).

- **Example 3:** Sam and Jane have $300,000 in combined resources just prior to the date Sam enters the nursing home. Sam will be eligible for Medicaid once the couple's combined assets have been reduced to $111,560 ($2,000 for Sam plus the maximum of $109,560 for Jane as her Community Spouse Resource Allowance).

Because States are allowed to have laws that are more generous than Federal law, some states automatically allow the Community Spouse to retain the maximum Community Spouse Resource Allowance.

Community Spouse Monthly Income Allowance. Each state allows a possible Community Spouse Monthly Income Allowance, which is a monthly income shift from the Nursing Home Spouse to the Community Spouse. Under Federal law, the Monthly Income Allowance ranges from the MMMNA (Minimum Monthly Maintenance Needs Allowance), currently $1,838.75 per month, to the maximum MMNA, currently $2,841.00 per month[6], and cannot exceed the maximum MMNA unless a court orders support in a greater amount. The Community Spouse Monthly Income Allowance is calculated as follows:

MMMNA (currently $1,838.75) + Excess Shelter Allowance

The Excess Shelter Allowance is the amount by which the Community Spouse's actual shelter expenses[7] exceed the state's "Shelter Standard" (also called the "Housing Allowance").

If the Community Spouse's actual monthly income is lower than the calculated Monthly Income Allowance, the shortfall can be made up from the income of the Nursing Home spouse. Ideally, this extra income will eliminate the need for the Community Spouse to dip into savings each month, which would result in gradual impoverishment.

EXAMPLE OF MONTHLY INCOME ALLOWANCE

Assume that Mary is the Community Spouse, that her sole source of income is $800 per month in Social Security benefits, and that her actual shelter expenses are $988. First we calculate the Excess Shelter Allowance as follows:

Actual Shelter Expenses	$988.00
Minus Shelter Standard	$-551.63
Equals Excess Shelter Allowance	$436.37

---

[6] These amounts are as of 2012, and are subject to change annually – for updated numbers, see the author's website at http://www.farrlawfirm.com/keyelderlawnumbers.htm. Most states use these numbers, sometimes rounded.

[7] Allowable expenses are: rent; mortgage (including interest and principal); taxes and insurance; condominium or cooperative fees; and the state's Utility Standard deduction, unless utilities are included in the community spouse's rent or condominium or cooperative fees.

Next, we calculate the MMNA as follows:

Minimum MMNA	$1,891.25
Plus Excess Shelter Allowance	$436.37
Equals MMNA	$2,327.62

Since Mary is entitled to a Monthly Maintenance Needs Allowance of $2,327.62, but only receives $800, she is entitled to receive the shortfall every month from John's Social Security check; this shortfall is called the Community Spouse Monthly Income Allowance.

MMNA	$2,327.62
Less actual income	$-800.00
Equals the Community Spouse Monthly Income Allowance	$1,527.62

The Community Spouse Monthly Income Allowance can be paid to Mary from John's income. The rest of John's income must be paid to the nursing home to partially cover the cost of his care.

chapter 12

MEDICAID ASSET PROTECTION BASICS

T he type of asset protection planning done by most experienced elder law attorneys is known by many names — it is most commonly called *Medicaid Asset Protection* or just *Medicaid Planning, but is also frequently referred to as Benefits-Focused Asset Protection, Long-term Care Planning, Life Care Planning, or Chronic Care Planning.*

WHAT IS THE GOAL OF MEDICAID ASSET PROTECTION PLANNING?

The goals that families have for doing Medicaid Asset Protection differ from person to person and family to family. However, it is most important to point out that preserving an inheritance for children is most often not the goal. On the contrary, generally for a married couple the most important goal is to ensure that the spouse remaining at home is able to live the remaining years of his or her life in utmost dignity, without having to

> *It is extremely important to point out that preserving an inheritance for children is typically **not the goal of Medicaid Asset Protection.***

suffer a drastic reduction in his or her standard of living. For a single or widowed client, the most important goal is typically to be able to enjoy the highest quality of life possible in the event of an extended nursing home stay. When there is an adult child or grandchild who is disabled, the primary goal is typically to protect assets to be used for the benefit of that disabled family member who is often also receiving Medicaid and Social Security Disability benefits.

Money that is protected through proper planning can be used to provide a nursing home resident with an enhanced level of care and a better quality of life while in a nursing home and receiving Medicaid benefits. For instance, protected assets can be used to hire a private nurse or a private health aide — someone to provide one-on-one care to the resident — to help the resident get dressed, to help the resident get to the bathroom, to help the resident at mealtime, and to act as the resident's eyes, ears and advocate.

Money that is sheltered through proper planning can also be used to purchase things for the nursing home resident or disabled child that are not covered by Medicaid — such as special medical devices, upgraded wheel chairs, transportation services, trips to the beauty salon, etc.

Lastly, a small percentage of clients do have a strong desire to leave a financial legacy for their children or grandchildren, particularly if there is a disabled child or someone who needs special financial help.

UNDERSTANDING EXEMPT ASSETS AND COUNTABLE RESOURCES

To qualify for Medicaid, applicants must pass some very strict tests on the type and amount of assets they can keep. To understand how Medicaid works, one first needs to learn to differentiate what are known as "exempt assets" from "countable assets." In Medicaid lingo, "countable assets" are technically referred to as "resources."

Exempt assets are those that Medicaid does not take into account. This generally includes:

- The applicant's principal residence, but only for the first six months of continuous institutionalization.[8]

---

[8] In Virginia, after the nursing home resident has been in the nursing home for six months of continuous institutionalization, the resident's home will become a countable resource unless the resident's spouse or other dependent relatives live in the home.

- Personal possessions, such as clothing, furniture, and jewelry;

- One motor vehicle, without regard to value;

- Property used in a trade or business;

- Certain prepaid burial arrangements;

- Term life insurance policies;

- A life estate in real estate (however, the transfer rules on life estates are very complicated and must be carefully observed);

- IRS Code d(4)(A) and d(4)© Special Needs Trusts; and

- Any assets that are considered inaccessible for one reason or another.

All other assets are generally "countable" assets, technically called "resources." Basically all money and property, and any item that can be valued and turned into cash, is a countable asset unless it is listed above as exempt. This includes:

> *All other assets are generally "countable" assets, technically called "resources." Basically all money and property, and any item that can be valued and turned into cash, is a countable asset unless it is specifically listed as exempt.*

- Cash, savings and checking accounts, credit union share and draft accounts;

- Certificates of deposit;

- U.S. Savings Bonds;

- Individual Retirement Accounts (IRAs), Keogh plans, 401(k) and 403(b) accounts;

- Nursing home accounts;

- Prepaid funeral contracts that can be canceled;

- Certain trusts (depending on the terms of the trust);

- Real estate other than the primary residence;

- Any additional motor vehicles;

- Boats or recreational vehicles;

- Stocks, bonds, or mutual funds; and

- Land contracts or mortgages held on real estate;

An unmarried applicant may have no more than $2,000 in "countable" assets in his or her name in order to be "resource eligible" for Medicaid.

Does this mean that if you need Medicaid assistance, you'll have to spend nearly all of your assets to qualify? No — there are dozens of Medicaid asset protection strategies that can be employed with the help of an experienced elder law attorney. These strategies will be explored in the next two chapters.

chapter 13

PRE-NEED MEDICAID PLANNING

T here are two general types of Medicaid Asset Protection Planning: Pre-Need Planning and Crisis Planning. This chapter will explain the former, and the following chapter will explain the latter.

Pre-need Medicaid Asset Protection Planning is for those persons planning well in advance of the need for nursing home care, while they are still healthy and typically still living independently. These are typically people who do not have long-term care insurance.

Many people erroneously think they can protect their nest eggs through estate planning using a traditional revocable living trust. Although a revocable living trust does a good job of avoiding probate when properly established and funded, an enormous limitation of a revocable living trust is that it does not protect assets whatsoever from creditors or from the expenses of long-term care. For those wishing to protect their assets from general creditors and from the expenses of long-term care, the primary planning option is the Living Trust Plus™ Asset Protection Trust.[9]

I created Living Trust Plus™ in 2006, and it's now being used by dozens of exceptional estate planning and elder law attorneys throughout the country, all of whom can be found listed on the website www.LivingTrustPlus.com. For purposes of Medicaid eligibility, the Living Trust Plus™ is the **only** type of asset protection trust that allows you to retain an interest in the trust

---

[9] *See* http://www.LivingTrustPlus.com.

while also protecting your assets from being counted against you by state Medicaid agencies.

Whereas the revocable living trust will protect your assets from probate, the Living Trust Plus™ is designed to protect your assets from probate PLUS lawsuits PLUS nursing home expenses. In my law firm, we call planning with a revocable living trust Level 2 Planning, and we call planning with the Living Trust Plus™ Level 3 Planning. You are a candidate for Level 3 Planning provided you are living independently and have no significant health problems that are likely to require nursing home care within the next five years.

Level 3 Planning offers you the peace of mind of knowing that the assets you place in trust:

- will be protected immediately from lawsuits and other general creditors;

- will be protected for Medicaid purposes (completely after five years, with partial protection possible in less than five years);

- may possibly be used by your beneficiaries to enhance your dignity and quality of life if and when you need nursing home care.

Whatever assets remain in your Level 3 Trust will, upon your death, be held for your beneficiaries, free of probate, in a sub-trust designed to protect each beneficiary's inheritance from lawsuits, divorce, and nursing home expenses of the beneficiary.

Your initial Level 3 investment with out firm includes free introductory enrollment in the Lifetime Protection Program™, our proprietary annual retainer plan that gives you, at no charge: an annual review and update of your existing documents (to accommodate changes in the law, changes in your family or financial circumstances, changes of address, or changes in your wishes); answers to questions that may arise about your documents; ongoing consultations as necessary and appropriate to continue to carry out your Asset Protection Plan; and ongoing annual registration with DocuBank. Provided you stay enrolled in our Lifetime Protection Program™, we will credit your initial Level 3 investment if you upgrade to Level 4 Planning, which will be discussed starting on page 66.

WHAT IS THE LIVING TRUST PLUS™?

The Living Trust Plus™ is an irrevocable asset protection trust that you create as part of your estate planning. The Living Trust Plus™ allows you to receive all ordinary income from the trust financial assets and to use any trust-owned realty or tangible personal property. The only restriction of the Living Trust Plus™ is you can have no direct access to principal (technically called the trust "corpus," which of course is Latin for "body"). If either you or your spouse has direct access to trust corpus, then all the assets in the trust would be deemed "countable" for Medicaid eligibility purposes and would be completely available to all other creditors. Prohibiting direct access to trust corpus is the key to why the Living Trust Plus™ works. Because you can't withdraw trust corpus, neither may your creditors.

> *Prohibiting direct access to trust corpus is the key to why the Living Trust Plus™ works. Because you can't withdraw trust corpus, neither may your creditors.*

HOW DOES THE LIVING TRUST PLUS™ WORK?

Despite the fact that you can't withdraw trust corpus, you have the ability to retain a very high degree of control over the Living Trust Plus™ assets. In addition to receiving all ordinary income from the trust, you can:

- Live in and use any trust-owned real estate.

- Sell any trust-owned real estate and have the trust purchase replacement real estate if desired.

- Use all trust-owned tangible personal property.

- Sell any trust-owned tangibles and have the trust purchase replacements if desired.

- Drive any trust-owned vehicles.

- Sell any trust-owned vehicles and have the trust purchase replacements if desired.

Additionally, you can:

- Serve as trustee of the Living Trust Plus™ if desired.

- Remove and replace someone else who's serving as trustee of the Living Trust Plus™.

- Change beneficiaries of the Living Trust Plus™ at any time during your life.

IS THE LIVING TRUST PLUS™ IRREVOCABLE?

Although the Living Trust Plus™ is an "irrevocable" trust, this simply means that you cannot unilaterally revoke the trust. Despite the fact that the trust is irrevocable, it can still be terminated so long as the trustee and all beneficiaries agree to terminate it. Many people, including many misinformed attorneys, erroneously think that the term "irrevocable" means the trust can never be revoked. But, in actuality, the term "irrevocable" means just one thing – that the trust cannot be unilaterally revoked by the trust creator. Although the Living Trust Plus™ is irrevocable and can't be revoked unilaterally by the trust creator, under common law and under the Uniform Trust Code, this type of irrevocable trust can be modified, revoked or partially revoked upon the consent of all interested parties, which is the trust creator, the trustee, and all trust beneficiaries.

WHAT IF I NEED SOME OF THE TRUST CORPUS?

Although direct withdrawal of trust corpus from the Living Trust Plus™ is prohibited, there's the potential to indirectly access the trust corpus in two ways. The first way is that the trustee has the ability to make distributions of trust corpus to the trust beneficiaries, who are typically your adult children. If the trustee distributes corpus to a trust beneficiary, that beneficiary can then voluntarily (without any pre-arrangement) return some or all of that corpus or use some or all of that corpus for your benefit. The second way for the settlor to possibly get at the trust corpus is for the trust to be terminated by the agreement of all interested parties as just explained.

Also, because The Living Trust Plus™ is designed to permit the trustee to make distributions to beneficiaries. Through this mechanism the trustee can stop income payments to a settlor who will be requiring Medicaid and can

> *The rainiest day possible is the day you wind up in a nursing home, so if you want to truly protect your nest egg and have it actually benefit you when the time comes, you need to do something to protect that money.*

avoid estate recovery in those states that use a broad definition of "estate."

WHAT KIND OF ASSETS SHOULD LIVING TRUST PLUS™ OWN?

The main types of assets that can be protected using the Living Trust Plus™ are real estate, including your primary residence, financial investments, ordinary bank accounts, and any life insurance that has cash value. Qualified retirement plans can't be owned by a trust, so to be protected they must first be liquidated and subjected to taxation. This is not necessarily a bad thing if you are over age 59 ½. Regardless of your political persuasion, Congress agreeing to keep taxes low while we are experiencing the highest debt and deficit in our country's history is implausible. Higher taxes are inevitably in our future until our country gets spending under control. Cash value in your retirement accounts is a countable asset for Medicaid, so the protect those assets by putting them into the Living Trust Plus™, they must be liquidated and subject to taxation. You can liquidate your retirement accounts now, while taxes are at historic lows, or wait until later and risk that the government will have changed the tax rate you have to pay when you withdraw the money. And don't forget that you WILL have to pay tax on this money. In fact, when you turn 70 ½, the government will force you start taking at least the required minimum distribution (RMD) each year and pay the prevailing tax rates at that time.

The Living Trust Plus™ doesn't affect your retirement income or your primary checking account.

WHY TO USE THE LIVING TRUST PLUS™

Medicaid Asset Protection. We live during a time when many baby boomers are taking care of their own parents and children, and consequently putting off planning for their own retirement and long-term care solutions. Furthermore, there are many Americans who can't qualify for long-term care insurance, and these are the ideal candidates for use of the true asset protection capabilities embodied by the Living Trust Plus™ Asset Protection Trust.

The typical clients who use the Living Trust Plus™ are in their mid-60s to mid-80s, already retired, and worried about the potential catastrophic cost of long-term care. They want to protect the nest egg that they've been saving for a rainy day.

Of course, as a Certified Elder Law Attorney, I know that the rainiest day possible is the day you wind up in a nursing home, so if you want to truly protect your nest egg and have it actually benefit you when the time comes, you need to do something to protect that money. For the vast majority of Americans, the Living Trust Plus™ is the best way to get this much-needed protection.

The Living Trust Plus™ is a means by which you can transfer the assets you wish to protect to a trust rather than directly to your children. Transfers to trusts can be rightfully viewed as protection, whereas transfers to adult children are outright gifts. Trusts provide a sense of dignity and security; gifts to children leave you at the mercy of your children and present or future any creditors of your children. Transfer to a Living Trust Plus™ are subject to the Medicaid five-year lookback period previously discussed on page 60.

Independence. By transferring assets to a Living Trust Plus™, income is paid directly to you rather than to your children, allowing you to maintain greater financial independence. When your real estate is transferred to a Living Trust Plus™, you retain the ability to live in the real estate or receive the rental income from the property.

Risk-Avoidance. If a parent transfers assets directly to his children, certain risks must be anticipated: creditors claims against a child; divorce of a child; bad habits of a child; need for financial aid; loss of step-up in basis.

A transfer to a Living Trust Plus™ avoids all of these risks.

TAXATION ISSUES RELATING TO THE LIVING TRUST PLUS™

Income Tax. Because all trust income flows through the trust to the settlor (also called the grantor), the Living Trust Plus™ is considered by the IRS to be a "grantor trust." Therefore, the ordinary income of the trust is paid directly to the settlor of the trust and the tax will be paid at the settlor's tax rate, rather than by the trust at the compressed trust tax rates.

Income Tax Reporting. The Rules for reporting income generated by assets owned by the Living Trust Plus™ are contained in the Instructions for Form 1041, under the section entitled "Grantor Type Trusts." The Living Trust Plus™ should obtain a separate tax identification number so that potential creditors, including Medicaid, will clearly see the trust as a separate entity. The trustee does not show any dollar amounts on the form itself dollar; amounts are shown only on an attachment to the form (typically called a Grantor Trust Statement) that the trustee or tax preparer files. The trustee should not use Schedule K-1 as the attachment nor issue a 1099.

> *The Living Trust Plus™ should obtain a separate tax identification number so that potential creditors, including Medicaid, will clearly see the trust as a separate entity.*

Gift Tax. Because the Living Trust Plus™ is designed so that the settlor retains a limited power of appointment in the trust corpus, transfers to the Living Trust Plus™ are not considered completed gifts for gift tax purposes.

Gift Tax Reporting. Even though the transfer of assets into the trust is not considered a taxable gift, pursuant to Treas. Reg § 25.6019-3 a Form 709, U.S. Gift Tax Return, should still be filed in the year of the initial transfer into the trust. On the Form 709, the transaction should be shown on the return for the year of the initial transfer and evidence showing all relevant facts, including a copy of the instrument(s) of transfer and a copy of the trust, should be submitted with the return. The penalty for not filing a gift tax return is based on the amount of gift tax due, so if there is no amount due there should be no penalty for failure to file. Nevertheless, a gift tax return should be filed pursuant to Treas. Reg § 25.6019-3. Additionally, the filing of a gift tax return could provide additional evidence to future creditors, including Medicaid, that a completed transfer was in fact made despite the fact that the transfer was not considered by the IRS to be a completed gift for tax purposes.

Gifts from the Trust. Although the transfer to the trust is an incomplete gift for gift tax purposes, if the trustee later distributes trust corpus from the trust to one or more of the beneficiaries, the tax result of such distribution is that a completed gift has now been made from the trust settlor to the beneficiary. Accordingly, a gift tax return should be filed by the settlor for the tax year of such distribution if the amount of such distribution exceeds the annual exemption amount.

Annual Exclusion Gifts. Under the current law, the Living Trust Plus™ can make an unlimited number of gifts to individuals of up to $13,000 per recipient, per year, and the settlor will not need to file a gift tax return.

Estate Tax. The corpus of the trust is taxable in the settlor's estate upon death under IRC Section 2036, which says that "[t]he value of the gross estate shall include the value of all property to the extent of any interest therein of which the decedent has at any time made a transfer . . . under which he has retained for his life . . . the possession or enjoyment of, or the right to the income from, the property . . . ."

Step Up in Basis. Because the Living Trust Plus™ is designed so that assets are included in the estate of the Settlor, the trust beneficiaries will receive a step up in tax basis as to trust assets to the fair market value of the assets as of the settlor's death.

Capital Gains Exclusion for Sale of Principal Residence. Since the settlor of the Living Trust Plus™ is considered the owner of the entire trust (including the residence) under IRS Grantor Trust rules, the Settlor is treated as the owner of the residence for purposes of satisfying the ownership requirements of § 121 of the Internal Revenue Code. Accordingly, by transferring a residence to a Living Trust Plus™, the exclusion from capital gains on the sale of a principal residence is maintained.

chapter 14

MEDICAID CRISIS PLANNING

Medicaid Crisis Planning is for families with a loved one who has already entered, or is about to enter, a nursing home, and it is expected that the nursing home resident will not be able to return home. If this described your family, you need to know that there are dozens of asset protection strategies that can be used, under the direct and ongoing supervision of a qualified and experienced elder law attorney, to protect your family's assets and obtain Medicaid benefits. In my law firm, we call Medicaid Crisis Planning "Level 4 Planning." This type of Planning provides comprehensive Medicaid Asset Protection, including completion and filing of the Medicaid application and all documents and actions required to obtain Medicaid. When eligible, Level 4 includes Veterans Benefits Planning and the filing of a Veterans Aid and Attendance Pension application at no charge. Under Level 4, we provide you with: a written Asset Protection Plan (APP); all appropriate asset protection documents; all research, conferences, advice, expertise, and other services necessary to achieve the desired goals; supervised execution of all documents required under the APP; and unlimited consultations between you and our attorneys and staff as necessary to design and implement the APP consistent with your needs, goals, and desires, and to carry out the APP to completion prior to our filing for Medicaid and/or Veterans Pension benefits.

HOW MUCH CAN BE PROTECTED?

If you're a married couple and one spouse is healthy and living at home, we can protect 100% of your assets, regardless of how the assets are titled. If you're not married, we can generally protect 40% to 70% of your assets. In addition to the Asset Protection under Level 4, we will assist you when needed with selection of care facilities, review all paperwork prior to signing, and represent you in connection with any threatened discharge from a care facility.

The asset protection strategies we use break down into two broad categories – Asset Purchase Strategies (also called "smart spenddown") and Asset Transfer Strategies.

A list of sample Asset Purchase Strategies and Asset Transfer Strategies is provided below.[10]

SAMPLE ASSET PURCHASE STRATEGIES AVAILABLE IN MOST STATES

- Prepayment of legal or other services;

- Payment for home improvements if home is exempt;

- Purchase of household goods and personal effects;

- Purchase of a more expensive home if the home is exempt;

- Purchase life estate and reside for one year;

- Purchase of pre-paid funeral arrangements;

- Purchase of a new car;

- Prepayment of taxes;

- Payment of outstanding debts;

- Purchase of a special Medicaid-compliant annuity.

---

[10]Most of these strategies are based on federal law, but none of these strategies should be attempted without the direct and ongoing supervision of an experienced and qualified elder law attorney who has both (1) a comprehensive understanding of each strategy's specific rules and requirements in your state and (2) a thorough understanding of each strategy's Medicaid, estate planning and tax consequences (including income tax and capital gains tax).

SAMPLE ASSET TRANSFER STRATEGIES AVAILABLE IN MOST STATES

- Transfer assets to blind or disabled child;

- Transfer assets to a trust for the sole benefit of a blind or disabled child;

- Transfer residence to caregiver child;

- Transfer residence to sibling on title for more than a year;

- Transfer residence subject to life estate;

- Transfer residence subject to occupancy agreement;

- Caregiver agreement between parent and child;

- Transfer and Cure.

chapter 15

WHY MEDICAID PLANNING IS ETHICAL

Medicaid Asset Protection is absolutely ethical and moral; in fact, it is the "right" thing to do if a family is concerned about the long-term care of a loved one. From a moral and ethical standpoint, Medicaid planning is no different from income tax planning and estate planning.

JUST LIKE INCOME TAX PLANNING

Income tax planning involves trying to find all of the proper and legal deductions, credits, and other tax savings that you are entitled to — taking maximum advantage of existing laws. Income tax planning also involves investing in tax-free bonds, retirement plans, or other tax-favored investment vehicles, all in an effort to minimize what you pay in income taxes and maximize the amount of money that remains in your control to be used to benefit you and your family.

JUST LIKE ESTATE PLANNING

Estate planning involves trying to plan your estate to minimize the amount of estate taxes and probate taxes that your estate will have to pay to the government, again taking maximum advantage of the existing laws. Similar to income-tax planning, estate planning is a way to minimize what your estate pays in taxes and maximize the amount of money that remains in your estate to be used to benefit your family.

Similarly, Medicaid planning involves trying to find the best methods to transfer, shelter, and protect your assets in ways that take maximum advantage of existing laws, all in an effort to minimize what you pay and maximize the amount of money that remains in your control to be used to benefit you and your family.

Like income-tax planning and estate planning, Medicaid planning requires a great deal of extremely complex knowledge due in part to constantly-changing laws, so you need to work with an experienced elder law attorney who knows the rules and can advise you properly.

JUST LIKE LONG-TERM CARE INSURANCE

For seniors over the age of 65, Medicaid has become equivalent to federally-subsidized long-term care insurance, just as Medicare is equivalent to federally-subsidized health insurance. Congress accepts the realities of Medicaid Planning through rules that protect spouses of nursing home residents, allow Medicaid Asset Protection via the purchase of qualified Long-Term Care Insurance policies, allow the exemption of certain types of assets, and permit individuals to qualify even after transferring assets to a spouse or to a disabled family members or to a caregiver child. To plan ahead and accelerate qualification for Medicaid is no different than planning to maximize your income tax deductions to minimize your income taxes. It is no different than taking advantage of tax-free municipal bonds.

JUST LIKE MAGIC

The "magic" that Elder Law attorneys are able to perform is not based on slight of hand. Elder Law attorneys do not "hide" assets. On the contrary, we provide total disclosure of everything we do to the relevant Medicaid agencies when we file the Medicaid application, as failure to provide full disclosure of all assets and all transfers would be a federal crime. The ways that Elder Law attorneys are able to shelter and protect assets may seem like "magic" to you, but that's only because you don't possess our legal knowledge and experience. It's the same with magicians -- the magic only appears to be "magical" because you don't know how

83

the trick is done. Just as magicians study and train for years to become good magicians, Elder Law attorneys also study and train for years to become experts in our field. To become a Certified Elder Law Attorney, attorneys must: spend an average of at least 16 hours per week practicing elder law during the three years preceding their application; must handle a minimum of 60 elder law matters, in 13 different areas of elder law, during those three years; participate in at least 45 hours of continuing legal education in elder law during the preceding three years; submit five references from attorneys familiar with their competence and qualifications in elder law; and must pass a full-day certification examination (one of the most recent exams had a 19% pass rate). Done with respect for the law and compassion for the elders that are being protected, Medicaid planning is not only ethically justified -- it is often imperative to the individual's quality of life.

OUR HEALTH CARE SYSTEM IS DISCRIMINATORY

Within the United States, no one yet has a right to basic long-term care. We give seniors virtually universal coverage for certain types of health problems. Treatment and surgery for health conditions such as heart disease, lung disease, kidney disease, bone disease, cancer, and hundreds of other medical conditions will not impoverish most seniors because Medicare and private health insurance cover these diseases, and we all pay our fair share for such coverage. But nighter Medicare nor private health insurance cover chronic illnesses such as Alzheimer's disease or other type of brain diseases causing dementia or loss of the ability to function independently. For these types of diseases, seniors must become officially "impoverished" under federal and state Medicaid rules in order to gain access to basic long-term care. Is this an ethical social policy that arbitrarily distinguishes among these different types of diseases? Is this an ethical social policy that provides full coverage for most diseases but forces elders with certain conditions to become impoverished in order to gain access to basic long-term care? Is it a surprise to anyone that most seniors will want to look for legal ways to preserve the efforts of their lifetime in order to protect themselves from this unfair and arbitrary social policy? Medicaid planning is not about "cheating" or "gaming" the system; it is about preserving a client's dignity and self-worth in the face of an unfair and arbitrary social policy. The ethical scandal is America's public policy, not the desire of seniors to avoid poverty.

chapter 16

MEDICAID CASE STUDIES

Though some families do spend virtually all of their savings on nursing home care, Medicaid laws do not require it. As outlined in the prior chapters, there are numerous legal and ethical strategies which can be used, with the assistance of an experienced (and preferably Certified) Elder Law Attorney, to protect family financial security. In this chapter, I will take you through several real-life case studies. First up will be a case study of the typical family who is completely unprepared for the worst-case scenario and does no planning whatsoever. Next we'll take a look at a family who prepared well in advance for a long-term care crisis, and then we'll study a couple and an individual who did last-minute planning but still were able to receive significant benefit. Please note that all of the following Case Studies represent "short version" scenarios. The kind of planning discussed in Case Studies 2, 3 and 4 must be handled in a very precise manner and should always be done with the assistance of an experienced elder law attorney.

CASE STUDY 1: JACK AND SARA – NO PLANNING

Sara and Jack had been married for 57 years when Jack, at age 81, suffered the first of several strokes. Jack spent 2 years in and out of hospitals and nursing homes for rehab after each stroke. Each time, Medicare, along with Jack's supplemental health insurance, paid for Jack's hospital and rehab stays because he always first spent at least 3 days in the hospital prior to going to the nursing home for short-term rehab. Each time Jack was discharged from short-term rehab, Sara would bring him home and take care of him.

Six months ago, the burden on Sara changed tremendously after

Jack had his third and worst stroke, which left him paralyzed on his left side and virtually bedridden, with severe brain damage causing about 80% loss of his short-term memory. Despite the doctor's recommendation to keep Jack in the nursing home for long-term care, Sara, who is age 82, diabetic, and herself slowing down greatly, brought Jack home to care for him because Sara thinks they can't afford the nursing home care, which the nursing home told her it is approximately $9,000 per month.

All Sara and Jack have in the way of assets is their paid-off house, worth about $400,000, and the remainder of Jack's IRA, which has about $100,000 left in it. As for their income, all they have is their respective Social Security income. Sara knows that Jack could be in the nursing home for many years, and that just one year in the nursing home could wipe out all of their money. If Jack were to be in the nursing for more than one year, she fears she'd have to sell their house to continue paying for Jack's care, and then where would she live? The nursing home admissions director told Sara that after spending all of their money, she could take out a reverse mortgage on their home and use the home equity to continue paying the nursing home, but this option also did not appeal to Sara. Fear and self-preservation kicked in for Sara – she could not help but worry about spending down their limited resources to provide nursing home care for Jack. These emotions joined with love for Jack and a desire to provide him with the best care, which she thought would be care from her, at their home.

WITH PLANNING

What Sara didn't know is that, with the help of a qualified Elder Law attorney, she could have protected all of their assets (the house and money) for herself and gotten Jack on Medicaid very quickly to pay for his nursing home care. Or Medicaid could have been used to pay for professional home health care for Jack, sparing Sara the tremendous burden of caring for Jack herself. Unfortunately, Sara had never heard of Elder Law, and instead went to see the Estate Planning attorney who had drawn up their Wills 15 years ago. All the Estate Planning attorney did was recommend that Jack sign a Power of Attorney and Advance Medical Directive naming Sara, and their son John as an alternate. He also recommended that Sara sign a Power of Attorney and Advance Medical Directive naming their son John, in case something happened to her. The Estate Planning attorney didn't know anything about Medicaid or asset protection, and so he didn't offer any relevant advice in that regard, and Sara didn't even know that there were vitally important questions she should be asking about Medicaid and Asset Protection.

So Sara purchased a hospital bed for Jack and set it up in the family room on the main level, in front of the television. With no concern for her own health, Sara has diligently cared for Jack at home for the past 12 months, but this caregiving has taken a huge toll on Sara, both mentally and physically. In addition to doing the things she's always done – shopping, cooking, cleaning, etc. – among her numerous additional duties Sara now has to change Jack's diapers and his soiled linens several times a day, do at least one extra load of laundry every day, keep track of and administer Jack's medications, hand feed Jack the special liquid diet that he must be on to avoid choking, and turn him several times a day so he doesn't develop bed sores.

Because Jack's needs are so severe, Sara has almost no time for herself. Sarah doesn't like to complain, but she has mentioned to her only son, John, that she's always tired, she's not able to get out to see her friends anymore, or to go to church (though she happily still mails in her weekly $100 contribution to the church offering to fulfill their annual pledge). She also confides in John that she cries a lot lately, and that she still worries incessantly about running out of money.

Two weeks ago, Sara fell in the bathtub because she was hurrying, as usual, so as not to leave Jack alone for too long. Sarah hit her head on the way down and lost consciousness.

Because neither Jack nor Sara were able to call 911, Sara lay in the bathtub, unconscious, for more than a day before their son, John (after calling and getting no answer for the better part of a morning), drove down on his lunch break to check on them. John found his father in his hospital bed, covered in his own feces and urine because his diapers hadn't been changed in almost two days; Jack was also dehydrated because he hadn't been fed during that time. He found his mother unconscious in the bathtub, and immediately thought she was dead.

Hysterical, John called 911 and the paramedics were there within a few minutes to deal with the situation.

After determining that Sara was alive but unconscious, the paramedics tried to revive her, but with no success. They transported Sara and Jack to the local emergency room, where Sara regained consciousness after 15 hours of observation in the ER. Upon regaining consciousness, Sara's pain was severe, as were her injuries – a severe concussion (which would lead to permanent brain damage and memory loss) a fractured right hip, a bone chip in her left hip, and a broken right arm.

Sara was never the same after this fall. Her memory loss from the brain damage was so bad that it mimicked advanced dementia, and the doctors at the hospital said there was nothing that could be done for her memory. They put a cast on her arm and sent her to the local nursing home for recovery and rehab.

As for Jack, after re-hydrating him at the hospital, he also was sent to the local nursing home for recovery and rehab.

Unfortunately, neither Sara nor Jack had been admitted for 3 days or more to the hospital, and neither Medicare nor their supplemental health insurance would pay for the recovery and rehab. The nursing home told their son, John, that he needed to sign the admission documents for both parents and start paying the $18,000 a month private rate, with the first month due in advance. John dutifully did what the nursing home told him, never stopping to consider if there was an alternative because, like his parents, he had never heard of Elder Law.

WITH PLANNING

What John didn't know is that, with the help of a qualified Elder Law attorney, he could have protected 40-70 percent his mother's assets (assuming they had already been 100% protected a year ago for Jack) and gotten Sara on Medicaid to pay for her remaining nursing home care.

About 3 months later, when John realized his parents were going to quickly run out of money, he listed their house for sale. Per the recommendation of the real estate agent, John listed the house for sale at $350,000. The tax assessed value of the house was $406,000, but the realtor said in her opinion the actual market value was between $317,000 and $350,000. When the house didn't sell within two months, John started to worry that it wasn't going to sell before his parents ran out of money, so John decided to buy the home himself for $317,000. To get the money to purchase his parent's house, John had to liquidate most of his retirement account and incur the income taxes and a 10% early withdrawal penalty, but he figured this was better than having to pay $18,000 per month for the care of his parents once their money ran out.

John put the proceeds from the sale of his parents' home in their bank account and continued to use this money to pay the nursing home bills.

About eighteen months later, Jack and Sara were still in the nursing home, and all of their money was gone. The nursing home told John he needed to apply for Medicaid for his parents. Without giving a single thought to hiring an attorney or even seeking legal advice, John applied for Medicaid as the nursing home told him to.

The first time John applied, even though he spent more than 25 hours over a weekend completing the Medicaid applications, both parents were denied Medicaid because John had failed to fill out the applications properly.

WITH PLANNING

With the help of an experienced Elder Law attorney, this result could have been avoided. Filing for Medicaid is one of the most complex and nightmarish endeavors in existence, and should never be undertaken without first consulting with an experienced Elder Law Attorney. In my firm, we fill out Medicaid applications for our clients every day to avoid the perils and pitfalls that people encounter when trying to file for Medicaid on their own.

The second time John applied, both parents were denied Medicaid again because John failed to provide the Medicaid agency with all of the documentation and verifications that they requested in connection with the sale of his parents' home and in connection with their charitable gifts, as the agency requested this at the last minute and John did not have time to hunt down and obtain the required documents.

WITH PLANNING

With the help of an experienced Elder Law attorney, this result could have been avoided. Our firm, for example, ensures that all required documentation is provided to us before we file the Medicaid application, so our clients don't have to routinely deal with last-minute document requests.

In the meantime, the nursing home bills were already piling up at the rate of $18,000 per month since Jack and Sara's money had run out, and the nursing home billing department was calling John at home and at work at least once a week, threatening to sue John for the outstanding nursing home bills if he did not make payment immediately. Finally they turned the outstanding bills ($54,000 for 3 months of nursing home care) over to a collection agency, which harassed John and threatened to destroy his credit.

At the same time John was receiving dunning notices from the collection agency, he was being told by the nursing home administrator that his parents were going to be discharged from the nursing home for failure to pay, and that it was John's responsibility to take them home and take care of them, as he had signed the nursing home contracts as the "Responsible Party" for both of his parents.

The third time John applied, he provided all of the requested documentation, and the Medicaid Agency finally approved Medicaid for both parents, but assessed a penalty period of 20 months. This penalty period was incurred because John's parents had made $26,000 in charitable gifts in the last 5 years, and had sold their house for $89,000 less than the tax assessed value (which Medicaid considers to be equivalent to a gift to the buyer of the home – in this case John – in the amount of $89,000). The total gifts of $115,000 were divided by the penalty divisor in their state, which was 5750, resulting in a 20-month penalty period, meaning a 10- month period of Medicaid ineligibility for each of his parents. This meant that although John's parents had no money left, Medicaid would not pay for their nursing home care for 10 months.

Who did have to pay for the nursing home during that time? According to the nursing home, John did, because he signed the nursing contract as the "Responsible Party" and because he was the recipient of the $89,000 gift in connection with the sale of the home. So John had to pay 10 months of nursing home costs for the care of his parents, at $18,000 per month. This was a total of

$180,000 that John had to pay as a penalty for trying to help his parents.

> **WITH PLANNING**
> With the help of an experienced Elder Law attorney, all of these bad results could have been avoided. The following Case Studies will demonstrate the benefits of proper planning.

CASE STUDY 2:   GLENDA – PLANNING IN ADVANCE

Three years ago Glenda's husband died after suffering a massive stroke. Although Glenda's husband had died quickly and had not needed to spend time in the nursing home after his stroke, Glenda has many friends whose spouses spent significant time in nursing homes prior to their death, and Jane knows, through these friends, of the financial devastation that is caused by prolonged nursing home stays. Although devastated over the loss of her husband, Jane is also glad that he did not have to spend any time in a nursing home, because she knows that a prolonged nursing home stay could have bankrupted her.

Although Glenda is 85-years old, she is still quite healthy, and able to live independently. The only thing that Glenda can't do is drive, because she has macular degeneration that is causing her eyesight to fail. Luckily, Glenda's oldest daughter, Jane, lives nearby and is retired, so Jane is able to take Glenda where she needs to go.

After the death of her father, one of the first places Jane takes her mom is to the attorney who did their estate planning documents years before her father had died, to see what needs to be done, if anything, about her father's estate. Jane and Glenda are happy to learn that only minimal work needs to be done because all of the assets of her parents were titled jointly, and would pass to Glenda automatically with proper notification of her husband's death.

Since they are at the lawyer's office, Glenda asks if there is anything that could be done to protect her assets against the possibility that she might some day need nursing home care. (Glenda's primary reason for wanting to do asset protection is to preserve her own future dignity and quality of life; she is not concerned about leaving a large inheritance to her children because all of her children are financially well-off in their own rights.) Although the lawyer is not a Living Trust Plus™ Attorney, he has heard of the Living Trust Plus™ and suggests that Glenda and Jane look into it as a method of accomplishing the asset protection they are interested in.

That evening, Jane helps Glenda look up the name of a Living Trust Plus™ Attorney by going to www.LivingTrustPlus.com, and they find that the Living Trust Plus™ Attorney in their area is offering an informational seminar the following weekend, so they sign up for seminar. At the seminar, Jane and Glenda learn all about the Living Trust Plus™ as a method of Medicaid Asset Protection (see page 72), and decide they wanted to pursue it further, so they make an appointment for a free consultation with the attorney.

Once the attorney confirms that Glenda is an appropriate candidate for the Living Trust Plus™, Glenda goes ahead and has the attorney prepare one for her, and Glenda also had the attorney transfer her house, which is mortgage-free, worth about $340,000 and is her major asset, into the Living Trust Plus™. Glenda decides that she will keep her $97,000 IRA, which is her only other significant asset, out of the trust.

For the next four years, Glenda remains relatively healthy, and is able to live day to day on her $1,200 per month retirement income plus minimum distributions from her IRA. Jane spends just 4 or 5 hours a week helping Glenda pay her bills and balance her checkbook, as her dad had always done that before his death, and driving Glenda to her medical appointments. On February 10, six days short of her 90th birthday, Glenda trips and falls and breaks her hip. After 3 days in the hospital and 4 weeks of rehab in a local nursing home, it becomes clear that Glenda needs to stay at the nursing home for long-term care.

Jane knows that her mom only has about $80,000 left in her IRA, and at $9,200 per month for the nursing home, Jane knows the IRA money will only last about another 10 months. Jane returns to the attorney who drew up Glenda's Living Trust Plus™ to see what can be done.

The attorney explains that Glenda should go ahead and use the remaining IRA money to pay for the first 10 months of nursing home care. Although the IRA distributions are subject to income tax, the tax incurred will be offset by Glenda's nursing home bills which qualify for the medical expense deduction, so little or no taxes will actually have to be paid.

During this 10-month period, Glenda's lawyer explains that Jane, as Trustee of her mother's Living Trust Plus™, should sell her mom's former residence. The $340,000 or so in proceeds from the sale of the former residence will go into Glenda's Living Trust Plus™ and Jane, as Trustee, can decide how to invest these proceeds – whether in CDs, mutual funds, stocks, bonds, etc.

At the end of this 10-month period, Glenda will not have any money left to pay for the nursing home. However, the lawyer explains that Jane, as Trustee of her mother's Living Trust Plus™, could then make a "back door" distribution of about $16,000 in trust assets as a gift to herself and then could, if she wishes, voluntarily use that gifted money to help her mother pay for the next two months of nursing home care. Assuming Jane were to do this, then at the end of said two month period, the Medicaid 5-year lookback period will have elapsed and the remaining $324,000 in her mother's Living Trust Plus™ will be protected from being counted when applying for Medicaid to pay the remaining nursing home bills for the rest of Glenda's life.

CASE STUDY 3: CRISIS PLANNING FOR A MARRIED COUPLE

Ralph and Betty, both age 82, were high school sweethearts who lived in a small town in Northern Virginia their entire adult lives. They purchased their modest-sized home for $22,000 in 1974 and now their home is worth about $250,000. Two weeks ago, their son, Mark, and their daughter, Mary, threw Ralph and Betty a surprise 60th anniversary party. Yesterday, Ralph, who has Alzheimer's, wandered away from home, as he had done several time before. The police found him, hours later, lying on the curb next to a local bus stop, talking incoherently about needing to get home to Pennsylvania (where he grew up as a child) because his mother (who had died 25 years ago) was expecting him for dinner. They took Ralph to the local hospital, where Ralph was diagnosed with a broken hip. Now the family doctor has told Betty that she needs to place Ralph in a nursing home. The nursing home closest to their house charges $320 per day — approximately $9,600 per month. Ralph and Betty grew up during the years after the Great Depression, and always tried to save something each month. Their financial assets (not including their real estate) are as follows:

Savings	$65,000.00
CDs	$135,000.00
Money Market	$67,000.00
Checking	$13,000.00
Total	$280,000.00

Ralph gets a Social Security check for approximately $1,000 each month; Betty's check is $450. Her eyes fill with tears as she tells me that Ralph's dad lived to age 95, and spent his last 7 years in a nursing home. Betty fears that if she has to pay $9,600 to the nursing home every month, which is over $115,000 per year, their entire life savings will be gone in a little over two years! And then she worries that she'll have to sell the home and that she and Mary (who is disabled and has been living with Ralph and Betty for over 10 years) will have nowhere to live. Mary requires significant assistance with her activities of daily living, and Betty has been the one primarily providing this care. Betty's also afraid she won't be able to pay her monthly bills because a friend told her that the nursing home will be entitled to all of Ralph's Social Security check. Most of Betty's fears are well-grounded, and if Mark had not been smart enough to do some research into Elder Law and come to my office, all of Betty's worst fears might have come true.

However, I have very good news for Betty and her children when they come to visit me. I explain that I can arrange for Betty to keep everything — all of their assets and all of their income — and still arrange for the Medicaid program to pay for Ralph's nursing home costs. This is because of special rules for married couples that allow a married couple to shelter all of their assets and, in many cases, all of their combined income, and still get the nursing home spouse on Medicaid. The exact strategies used to protect assets are extremely complicated and vary depending on the situation, but there are dozens of different Medicaid Asset Protection strategies available, and in any given case an experienced Elder Law Attorney will use between 4 and 8 of those dozens of strategies. During one of our meetings, Betty mentions that she has a younger sister, Celia, who just lost her husband to cancer. Betty tells me that Celia has no children of her own, and that Celia and Betty and Betty's kids have always been very close. Given that Celia is now living alone, I suggest that Betty consider inviting Celia to come live with her and Mary in Betty's home, and having Celia purchase an interest in Betty's home with the proceeds from the sale of Celia's home. Betty and Celia love this idea, and my office eventually helps them handle the purchase and re-titling process of Betty's home. Besides the wonderful companionship that Celia provides for Betty and

Mary, Celia also makes Betty's life much easier because Celia helps provide care for Mary.

CASE STUDY 4: CRISIS PLANNING FOR A SINGLE OR WIDOWED INDIVIDUAL

Four years later (a year after Ralph's death), Betty has a stroke that lands her in a nursing home. Betty's sister, Celia, and Betty's children, Mark and Mary, come to visit me – distraught over Betty's stroke and in a financial panic because they fear that they will have to spend all of Betty's assets to pay for her nursing home care and then they fear the home will need to be sold, leaving Celia and Mary homeless. Mark has a very good job and is financially secure, so his goal is the same as Celia and Mary's goal -- to keep the house in the family for Celia and Mary to live in and to protect Betty's assets so they can be used to (1) preserve Betty's quality of life and dignity and (2) care for Mary to also preserve Mary's quality of life to the greatest extent possible.

Betty still has most of the assets that were protected in Case Study 3, though she has spent about $50,000 repairing and fixing up her house to make it more accommodating for her and Celia and Mary:

House	$250,000.00
Savings	$65,000.00
CDs	$85,000.00
Money Market	$67,000.00
Checking	$13,000.00
Total	$480,000.00

She has her Social Security income, and Ralph's survivor benefit income, but this income is still not nearly enough to afford the monthly cost of nursing care. She's afraid that her home will have to be sold and all of the proceeds spent to pay for her nursing home care. Although this is what the Medicaid Agency will tell her, I am pleased to tell them that there are numerous legal and ethical ways to protect Betty's assets and get her qualified for Medicaid.

First, I explain that we can protect the house in two different ways: we can either transfer Betty's interest in the home to her sister, Celia, or to a trust for the benefit of her daughter, Mary. Normally, giving away your interest in a house would cause a transfer penalty (see page 61), but there are some exceptions to this rule. One exception is that you can transfer your home to a sibling who has an equity interest in your home and has resided in your home for at least one year immediately before entering a nursing home. Another exception is that you can transfer your home to a special type of trust established for the benefit of a disabled child. There are many legal and factual considerations to be made before determining the best strategy or combination of strategies to use, and the implementation of either strategy must be done in compliance with strict Medicaid rules but, needless to say, Celia and Betty's children are thrilled with this news.

After protecting the house using one of these strategies, Betty will still have the remaining financial assets to be dealt with:

Savings	$65,000.00
CDs	$85,000.00
Money Market	$67,000.00
Checking	$13,000.00
Total	$230,000.00

Can any of these financial assets also be protected? The answer, again, is very good news for Betty's children. They can actually protect ALL of Betty's assets! How? Much of the money can be protected by purchasing exempt assets: they can protect about $20,000 of the money by purchasing certain federal savings bonds in Betty's name; about another $20,000 can be used to purchase prepaid funeral arrangements for both Betty and Mary; about

$50,000 can be used to purchase a wheelchair accessible van that will help Celia drive both Betty and Mary around in the future. The rest of the money can be protected by transferring it to a special type of trust established for the benefit of Mary because Mary is Betty's disabled child. All of these asset protection strategies are extremely complicated to implement correctly, and should therefore always be done under the supervision of an experienced elder law attorney, but the bottom line in this particular case is that all of Betty's assets can be legally and ethically protected.

chapter 17

FREQUENTLY ASKED QUESTIONS ABOUT MEDICAID

Question: Is it *legal* to transfer or retitle assets in an attempt to qualify for Medicaid?

Answer: Yes, it is absolutely legal. There are no laws prohibiting the transfer or re-titling of assets. However, transfers must be made very carefully, because a Medicaid applicant who has made uncompensated transfers within 5 years of applying for Medicaid will face a "penalty period" for Medicaid based on the amount of the transfer divided by the average cost of a month of nursing home care in the applicant's geographic area. See page 61 for a more detailed explanation if how the transfer penalty period is calculated.

Question: If someone transfers assets, when does the Medicaid "period of ineligibility" start — when the transfer is made or when the applicant applies for Medicaid?

Answer: The "period of ineligibility" begins when the applicant applies for Medicaid and is approved for Medicaid *but for* the application of the period of ineligibility.

Question: How much of my assets can be protected if I have not done any planning in advance?

Answer: This varies from client to client and depends on the situation and the specific goals and desires of the client and the client's family. In general, if you're married, we can protect 100% of your assets, regardless of how the assets are titled. If you're not married, we can generally protect 40% to 70% of your assets.

Question: I've heard you can't do Medicaid planning within five years of entering a nursing home — is this true?

Answer: No. This is a myth. As we have already stated, the law imposes a calculated period of ineligibility for certain types of transfers made prior to applying for Medicaid; however, an experienced elder law attorney will be mindful of these laws and will be careful to comply fully with and work within the law, sometime even making transfers intentionally to create a period of ineligibility. Plus, there are several different planning strategies that can be implemented at any time — even after someone has already entered a nursing home — and will not trigger any period of ineligibility. Because of the complexities of this type of planning, many of the strategies used and transfers made as part of a Medicaid plan are often very time sensitive, and you must always be sure to follow your attorney's instructions carefully.

Question: If I added a child's name to my bank account more than 5 years ago, is it now protected from having to be spent for the nursing home?

Answer: No. The entire amount in a joint bank account is still counted as belonging to you unless you can prove some or all of the money was actually contributed by the child whose name is on the account. Moreover, joint ownership with children can be disastrous for a number of reasons unrelated to Medicaid transfer rules. For example, your accounts, once in joint ownership with a child, will be vulnerable to the debts and liabilities of that child. Thus, if your child is in an automobile accident, your property could be at risk; or if your child has a business setback, runs up large debts, or goes through a bankruptcy or divorce, your home will be at risk. Also, because jointly-owned assets will pass directly to the co-owner when you die, and not through your Will or Trust, titling assets in joint ownership may unintentionally disinherit your other children.

Question: Can't I just give all of my assets away?

Answer: The answer is "maybe" — but only if you do it the right way and at the right time. If assets are given away at the wrong time and/or in the wrong amount, the law provides for a penalty —

a period of ineligibility for Medicaid — based on the amount of the transfer. See page 61 for a more detailed explanation if how the transfer penalty period is calculated.

Question: Doesn't federal law allow me to give away $10,000 per year to my children?

Answer: Yes. In fact, the tax limit has gone up to $13,000 — the Federal Gift Tax laws allow you to give away up to $13,000 per year to anyone you want. You and your spouse may each give an unlimited number of these $13,000 gifts per year. So, for example, if you have 4 children and 8 grandchildren, you could give away up to $156,000 each year ($13,000 x 12) if you each gave $13,000 to each child and grandchild. However, even though the Federal Gift Tax laws allow you to give away up to $13,000 per year to as many people as you wish *without gift tax consequences*, Medicaid laws still apply to these gifts, meaning that these gifts will result in a penalty period for Medicaid. For example, assuming you live in a state with an $8,000 penalty divisor as shown in the example on page 61, your $156,000 annual gift would result in a Medicaid penalty period of 19.5 months ($156,000 / $8,000).

Question: Does giving money to my church or other charities create a penalty?

Answer: Yes. Giving away money to charity is treated the same as giving away money to your children or grandchildren. Many people who apply for Medicaid are horrified to discover that they are penalized for having been good stewards and having given money to charities. There is no exception for gifts made to charity, though some states do have exceptions for small amounts that are made on a regular basis.

Question: Are there any assets that can be transferred without resulting in a period of ineligibility?

Answer: Yes. There are transfers to certain recipients that will not trigger a period of Medicaid ineligibility. These exempt recipients include:

(1) A spouse (or anyone else for the spouse's benefit);

(2) A blind or disabled child;

(3) A trust for the benefit of a blind or disabled child; or

(4) A trust for the benefit of a disabled individual under age 65 (even for the benefit of the applicant under certain circumstances).

Question: Are there any special rules that apply to the transfer of a family home?

Answer: Yes. There are special exceptions that apply with regard to the transfer of a family home. In addition to being able to make the transfers without penalty to one's spouse or blind or disabled child, or into trust for other disabled beneficiaries, the applicant may freely transfer his or her home to:

(1) A child under age 21 (though transferring to a child under 18 can be very dangerous);

(2) A sibling who has lived in the home during the year preceding the applicant's institutionalization and who already holds an equity interest in the home; or

(3) A "caretaker child," defined as a child of the applicant who lived in the house for at least two years prior to the applicant's entry into a nursing home and who during that period provided such care that the applicant did not need to move to a nursing home. Very strict proof requirements are needed to obtain this exception.

Question: Can I really be forced to sell my home in order to qualify for Medicaid?

Answer: Yes — without proper advance planning, many Medicaid applicants find themselves forced to sell their homes in order to qualify for Medicaid. Fortunately, there are many ways to protect the equity in a home, but since the Medicaid rules are complex and constantly changing, you will need to seek help from an experienced elder law attorney to help you in your planning.

chapter 18

MOVING YOUR LOVED ONE

Most nursing home admissions for long-term care take place after a stay at the nursing home for short-term rehabilitation. As explained on page 36, if your loved one has three-day hospital stay and is then admitted directly from the hospital into a skilled nursing facility for short-term rehabilitation, then Medicare should pay the full cost of the nursing home stay for the first 20 days, and may continue to pay part of the cost of the nursing home stay for the next 80 days. If your loved one can not be adequately cared for at home after this short-term rehabilitation stint, then your loved one needs long-term care and can stay at the same facility and move seamlessly from short-term rehab into long-term care, or can be moved, if desired (and if you can find another facility willing to accept your loved one), to a different facility for long-term care. Keeping your loved one at the same facility is **much simpler**, as you don't need to worry about finding a facility willing to accept your loved one, as the facility he or she is in has already accepted your loved one, and finishing rehab is not grounds for discharging a patient.

In fact, there are very limited reasons why a nursing facility can discharge a patient. These are detailed under 42 CFR Section § 483.12 (a)(2):

> (I) The transfer or discharge is necessary for the resident's welfare and the resident's needs cannot be met in the facility;

> (ii) The transfer or discharge is appropriate because the resident's health has improved sufficiently so the resident no longer needs the services provided by the facility;

(iii) The safety of individuals in the facility is endangered;

(iv) The health of individuals in the facility would otherwise be endangered;

(v) The resident has failed, after reasonable and appropriate notice, to pay for (or to have paid under Medicare or Medicaid) a stay at the facility. For a resident who becomes eligible for Medicaid after admission to a facility, the facility may charge a resident only allowable charges under Medicaid; or

(vi) The facility ceases to operate.

First, plan the nursing home admission carefully. If you know the resident becomes very difficult to deal with in the late afternoon, plan the admission for mid-morning. Next, complete the admission paperwork before your loved one actually moves into the facility. This will allow you to spend the first few hours they are there with them, getting them settled and making them feel secure in their new living environment.

Bring along some familiar items for the resident, so that his or her room will feel more like home (but keep in mind that space is limited, especially in a semi-private room). Mark every piece of clothing with a permanent laundry marker. When a facility is washing clothes for 120 people, things occasionally end up in the wrong room, but that is less likely if the item is properly marked. If you are going to do your loved one's laundry, post a sign on the closet door to notify staff, and provide a laundry bag or basket where dirty clothes can be placed.

Keep in mind that the staff of the facility is just meeting your loved one for the first time. They do not know his or her likes or dislikes, or those little nuances that make providing care go more smoothly. The best way you can help your loved one is to tell the staff, in writing, as much information as possible about your loved one, including his or her likes and dislikes, typical daily schedule, pet peeves, and so on.

Get to know the people who are caring for your loved one. Most important, stay involved. Let everyone know how much you care and how committed you are to your loved one's care. Also understand you will not help your loved one by becoming anxious or emotional. Assure him or her that although this is not an ideal situation, you will be there to make it as painless as possible.

Once the facility has been chosen, there are numerous steps you can take and professionals you can call on to make the moving process less traumatic for you and your loved one.

ORGANIZING AND DECLUTTERING

For many seniors and their families, the task of sifting through boxes and mountains of paperwork and deciding what the keep and what to toss is overwhelming. There are many Professional Organizers who specialize in helping seniors organize and declutter their homes. You can find a Professional Organizer through the Web site of the National Association of Professional Organizers at www.napo.net.

After a lifetime of accumulation, many seniors will need assistance from a junk removal service such as 1-800-Got-Junk? at www.1800gotjunk.com or College Hunks Hauling Junk at www.1800JunkUSA.com.

RETAINING RECORDS

For future Medicaid purposes, be sure to retain all financial records for at least the five years, and keep all records regarding joint ownership and regarding the sale or acquisition of real estate forever. For help sorting through and organizing financial and legal records, you may want to hire a Daily Money Manager. These professionals provide personal financial/bookkeeping services to senior citizens, the disabled, and even busy professionals. You can find a Daily Money Manager at the Web site of the American Association of Daily Money Managers at www.aadmm.com.

MANAGING THE MOVE

As with other aspects of the move, there are professionals – called Senior Move Managers – who specializing in helping older adults transition from their long time family home to alternative living arrangements. Senior Move Managers can help with sorting and packing the client's personal possessions, space planning, hanging pictures, organizing estate sales, and distributing tangible items to charities and adult children.

You can find a Senior Move Managers at the Website of the National Association of Senior Move Managers at www.nasmm.org.

SELLING THE HOME

Once you have decluttered, organized, and decided what to keep and what to trash, it's most likely time to sell the home. Before you sell the home, be sure to talk with a qualified Elder Law Attorney because there are specific Medicaid requirements that must be followed when selling a home within 5 years of applying for Medicaid. Failure to follow these requirements can lead to unforseen penalties and other hardships.

For help actually selling the home, consider engaging a real estate agent who is certified as a Seniors Real Estate Specialist® – these are real estate agents who specialize in senior needs and can help ease the transition. You can find a Seniors Real Estate Specialist® at www.seniorsrealestate.com. Your real estate agent may also recommend hiring a staging professional who can make modifications that will best showcase your house and make it appeal to the broadest audience possible. You can also find an Accredited Staging Professional at www.stagedhomes.com.

chapter 19

HOW TO GET THE BEST POSSIBLE CARE

Once you find a nursing home placement for your loved one, you can begin the process of easing the transition from one level of care to another. If you have been providing some or all of your loved one's care, you will notice a change in your role. Rather than functioning as a caregiver, you will become a care advocate. You will still be caring for your loved one, but in a new way.

Your key roles will be to participate in planning your loved one's care, communicating frequently with the facility staff, and ensuring that your loved one gets the best possible care in the new environment. If your loved one has assets set aside that have been properly protected using some of the techniques discussed in the previous chapter, these assets can now be used to enhance the level and quality of care that will be provided to your loved one. You can use these protected assets to hire a private sitter or a Geriatric Care Manager, to purchase the best medical equipment, and to hire the best doctors for your loved one.

CARE PLANNING

Federal law requires every long-term care facility to create a care plan. The care plan begins with a baseline assessment, which should occur within two weeks after a resident moves into the new facility, by a team from the nursing home (which may include a doctor, nurse, social worker, dietician, and physical, occupational, or recreational therapist). This team will use information provided by the resident and the family about the resident's medical and emotional needs to generate this baseline assessment, which then becomes the yardstick against which the caregivers can measure the resident's progress.

You can help by making a list of your loved one's medical, psychological, spiritual, and social needs, as well as his or her preferences and usual routine. For example, you might give the staff the following type of information: "Dad likes to listen to classical music on the radio as he falls asleep" or "Mom's always been a night-owl; she goes to sleep at around 1 a.m. and wakes up at 10am." You should also note signs of depression, or symptoms of dementia. Since the assessment team does not know your loved one as well as you do, your input may be invaluable, especially if the resident is not able to provide meaningful input. Although development of a care plan is something required to be done by a nursing home, a care plan can, and ideally should, be created in advance, well before the need for nursing home care. By planning in advance, when you have a clear mind and the ability to communicate effectively, you can much better guarantee that your wishes, lifestyles and desires are documented and will be communicated to your future caregivers, whether these be family members, private nurses, home health aides, or staff in a nursing home.

The easiest way to develop your own care plan is to use a tool such as the Lifestyle Care Plan, created by Advance Care Planning, Inc. The Lifestyle Care Plan is a proprietary document that is created by special software that gathers, organizes, stores and disseminates information provided by you in an interview, in order to better serve your future healthcare needs and to guide those who you will depend or for future care. The Lifestyle Care Plan identifies your specific needs, desires, habits and preferences and guides your caregiver in a unique manner. A Lifestyle Care Plan should be created as part of your basic Estate Plan or as part of your Long-Term Care Plan, because the best person to create a care plan for you is you. The following example is provided by Advance Care

Planning, Inc. of how an Lifestyle Care Plan can help improve a day in the life of Lynn, a typical nursing home resident:

Lynn, at the age of 85, has been placed in the nursing home due to a stroke. She is incontinent, but if taken to the restroom at appropriate times she will be continent most of the time. She is alert, but somewhat confused at times. She very much knows what she wants but cannot always verbalize it. She is able to feed herself finger foods.

Without an Lifestyle Care Plan	With an Lifestyle Care Plan
5:30 AM: Awakened. Hospital gown taken off, given some quick care, dressed for the day in someone else's house dress. It is a pretty house dress, but she does not like house dresses.	7:00 AM: Awakened. Taken to the bathroom for quick morning care, then placed in a comfortable chair in her room in front of the TV with a requested show on to await breakfast. Stays in her short PJ's and a robe since it is a shower day.
7:30AM: Taken to the dining room for breakfast. Given one cup of coffee, not offered more coffee. Not served bacon due to her high cholesterol.	7:30AM: Served bacon and eggs for breakfast. Her cholesterol is high, but she stated her wishes to eat a regular diet, including bacon and eggs for breakfast, in her Lifestyle Care Plan. She has two cups of coffee, as she has done for the last 65 years.

After Breakfast: Taken to sit in the hallway outside of her room.	After Breakfast: Taken to the bathroom and then to shower room. Her hair is washed, as it is with every shower per her Lifestyle Care Plan. She prefers to shower in the morning. After shower, dressed in her navy blue jogging suit with her red tee shirt, per her Lifestyle Care Plan.
1-2 hours Later: Taken to her room, has her brief changed and then is set in the hallway by the nurse's station. Her lips were not moistened, nor does she have access to chapstick.	1-2 Hours Later: Has her chapstick around her neck and is able to put it on herself frequently. Though her lips do not look dry, they feel dry to her. Her Lifestyle Care Plan notes that the staff should help her moisten her lips frequently.
10:00 AM: Given six pills – two for high cholesterol, one for irregular heartbeat, one for hiatal hernia to prevent heart burn, one for hypertension and one for arthritis.	10:00 AM: Given three pills – one for hiatal hernia to prevent heartburn, one for hypertension and one for arthritis. Decided in her Lifestyle Care Plan that if she ever entered a nursing home she would prefer not to take the other medications.

11:00 AM: Still sitting in the hall by the nurse's station.	11:00 AM: Taken outside to sit in the shade. She does not like crafts, but prefers to be outside in the shade, weather permitting.
12:00 Noon: Taken to the dining room for lunch. Given a lean hamburger, no salt allowed, a salad with lowfat dressing and applesauce. Needs assistance with the applesauce.	12:00 Noon: Taken back to her room for lunch; placed in her chair in front of the TV with her program of choice. Given a cheeseburger, packets of salt, french fries and apple slices. Her Lifestyle Care Plan states that she does not want to be spoon-fed and would prefer finger foods.
After Lunch: Taken to the nurse's station to sit in the hallway.	After Lunch: Taken to the restroom and then placed in her recliner to rest and watch her favorite movie on her DVD player.
2:00 PM: Placed in bed to have brief changed, and rest.	2:00 PM: Still watching her movie.
3:30 PM: Placed in wheelchair and taken to ceramics class.	3:30 PM: Gets her weekly manicure instead of going to ceramics class. She does not like crafts.
5:00 PM: Taken to room to have brief changed.	5:00 PM: Taken to the restroom. Prepared for dinner.

5:30 PM: Taken to dining room for dinner. Served chicken. Lynn loves hot dogs but they are not served to her due to her high cholesterol.	5:30 PM: Placed in her chair in her room for dinner. Served hot dogs with green pepper slices, cherry tomatoes and veggie dip. Enjoyed a brownie for dessert.
After Dinner: Taken to the nurse's station to sit in the hall. There is a TV with DVD at the nurse's station; staff puts a movie on for those sitting in the hall to watch. The movie is one which Lynn has seen several times and does not like.	After Dinner: She continues to watch TV until 7:30 PM.
8:30 PM: Taken to the shower. She prefers to bathe in the morning.	7:30 PM: Taken to the bathroom and helped to prepare for bed. She wears her short pajamas per her Lifestyle Care Plan.
After Shower: Dressed in a hospital gown and put to bed with one pillow at her head.	8:00 PM: Placed in bed with a talking book. It is a legal mystery, the type of book she likes. She has stated in her Lifestyle Care Plan that she likes to go to bed by 8:00 PM to read. She is only able to make use of talking books at this time.

The room is 75 degrees and she is very warm. She throws her covers off since she is too warm to sleep. The staff does come in and turn her several times. They place her on her back (she has never been able to sleep on her back) and they always cover her back up. Her brief is changed once during the night.	In bed, she has down pillows (5 ft.) on either side of her, between her legs, and 3 at her head, as she has slept for 40 years. The room temperature is 70 degrees, which is slightly warm for her. The temperature cannot be adjusted due to her roommate, so her personal fan is turned on to keep her cooler. She sleeps well but is awakened by the staff twice to take her to the toilet, per her Lifestyle Care Plan. She remains continent at night.
The following day, she falls asleep in her chair by the nurse's station since she did not sleep well the night before. Her children come to take her out to lunch but she appears too sleepy so she does not go.	The following day she is rested and has a strong sense of well-being. Her children come and take her to lunch. She is gone several hours, and rests in her chair for two hours upon her return.

If you have not created an Lifestyle Care Plan prior to entering a nursing home, the assessment team at the nursing home will gather information from your friends and family members to develop a care plan. The formal care plan defines specific care the resident needs and outlines strategies the staff will use to meet them. The assessment team meets during the first month of a new resident's placement at a care planning meeting. Family members, as well as the resident, may attend. When you go to the care plan meeting, bring along a copy of the list of needs you gave the assessment team earlier. Together, you can discuss your loved one's needs and the care plan the team has developed. If some need has been overlooked, you can ensure that the assessment team addresses it during this meeting.

The formal care plan becomes part of the nursing home contract. It should detail the resident's medical, emotional and social needs and spell out what will be done to improve (when possible) or maintain the resident's health.

Federal law requires that nursing home care result in improvement if improvement is possible. In cases where improvement is not possible, the care must maintain abilities or slow the loss of function. For example, if your mother has a slight problem with language when she moves into the nursing home, the care plan should include activities that encourage her use of language unless or until the disease's progression changes this ability.

Federal law also requires that nursing homes review the resident's care plan every three months and whenever the resident's condition changes. It must also reassess the resident annually. For example, if your father had bladder control when he entered the nursing home, but has since become incontinent, this significant change in his status means the nursing home staff must develop a new care plan that addresses his new need.

As a care advocate, you'll want to monitor your loved one's care to be sure the nursing home is providing the care outlined in the care plan. You should also attend all care planning meetings, whether regularly scheduled or when held because of a change in your loved one's health. By being as involved as possible with the care planning process, you will help to ensure that your loved one gets the best possible care while in the nursing home.

chapter 20

THE RIGHTS OF NURSING HOME RESIDENTS

Residents of nursing homes enjoy the same constitutional and civil rights they had when they were living in their own homes. In fact, residents are protected by state and federal laws which recognize their vulnerability. Residents and family members should become familiar with these laws to make certain their rights are being protected.

All nursing homes that accept Medicare or Medicaid are required to comply with the Nursing Home Reform Act.[11] This law was enacted to ensure that nursing home residents "attain or maintain the highest practicable physical, mental and psychosocial well-being." In addition to this federal act, most states have their own set of regulations governing the rights of nursing home residents and residents of assisted living facilities. Taken together, the federal Nursing Home Reform Act and your state statutes provide a sweeping "Bill of Rights" for all residents of nursing homes and assisted living facilities, whether receiving federal funds or private-pay. The following is a summary of the important protections under the federal Nursing Home "Bill of Rights":

THE RIGHT TO MAKE DECISIONS

Nursing home residents may exercise their rights as citizens without interference from the nursing home. Nursing home residents have the right to make financial and medical decisions -- including the right to check out of the nursing home — unless the resident has

---

[11] The Nursing Home Reform Act, part of the Omnibus Budget Reconciliation Act of 1987.

chosen, in advance, who will assert his or her rights if the resident is no longer able to do so (via a financial and/or health care power of attorney) or if a court has appointed someone to make those decisions (guardianship/conservatorship).

THE RIGHT TO BE FULLY INFORMED

Upon admission to a facility, a residents is entitled to information about the rights of residents of the facility. Each resident must be informed orally and in writing of those rights. Residents have the right to be informed of the services offered and charges for those services (including those not covered by the facility's daily rate); residents are entitled to know the facility's regulations, the results of state inspections, the procedures for transfer, and the names and addresses of every owner of the facility.

Residents have the right to be informed of their medical condition and treatment plan. Residents have the right to receive notice of changes concerning their treatment, including but not limited to altering medications, a change in physical or mental status, room or roommate changes, and a transfer or discharge from the nursing home. In addition, if a nursing home changes its charges or services, it is required to notify the residents, in writing, at least 30 days before the change goes into effect.

THE RIGHT TO PARTICIPATE IN CARE PLANNING

Residents have the right to full participation in their care planning — including the right to refuse services and the right to refuse medical treatment. Residents have the right to participate in their own care plan meetings (and invite anyone they wish to attend those meetings, as well). Residents must be able to choose their own doctor and choose a pharmacy (so long as the pharmacy's unit dose system is the same as the nursing home's). Unless the attending physician or interdisciplinary team has determined it unsafe, each resident has the right to self-administer his or her medications.

Residents have the right to inspect their charts and may, upon written request, obtain copies of all of their own records. Residents have the right to information regarding how to examine those records, as well.

THE RIGHT TO BE TREATED WITH DIGNITY AND RESPECT

One of the most fundamental rights, and also one of the most overlooked, is the legal right residents have to be treated with dignity and respect. So long as it is not detrimental to their care plan, residents have the right to make their own schedules and choose which activities they attend. In making their own schedules, residents have the right to decide what time they wake up in the morning, what time they eat their meals and what time they go to bed at night.

Residents have the right to be addressed in the manner they choose — whether by a formal title — such as Mr. Smith, Mrs. Jones, Dr. Baker or General Johnson — or by a first name or a nickname if that is their preference.

THE RIGHT TO CONFIDENTIALITY

All information regarding personal, financial, medical and social affairs is privileged and is to be kept confidential. The nursing home may not show the resident's chart to other people or agencies without permission, nor may they discuss treatment options with others unless they have permission.

THE RIGHT TO PRIVACY

Residents have the right to privacy in all aspects of life. They have the right to meet privately with any visitors (family, friends, physician, ombudsman, legal representative or anyone else), to send and receive private, unopened mail, and to make private telephone calls. Residents have the right to have all medical and personal care provided with privacy, using visual barriers to prevent others from viewing care and treatment. Residents have the right to perform all bodily functions (bathing, toileting, etc.) in private. If assistance is required, only those staff members needed to help should be present. Subject to possible restrictions based on care needs or payor source, residents have the right to take trips out of the facility for lunch or dinner, for a family holiday, or for a weekend visit.

THE RIGHT TO VOICE GRIEVANCES

Every nursing home must have a system to address concerns relating to residents' treatment or care. This includes grievances residents have concerning the behavior of other residents. Residents have the right to prompt efforts for resolution by the nursing home. The staff and administration are prohibited by law from retaliation for complaints. The nursing home must also post information relating to pertinent government and advocacy organizations (such as the number and address for the Long Term Care Ombudsman). Residents, of course, maintain the right to report crimes to the local police and/or district attorney.

THE RIGHT TO MANAGE FINANCES

Residents have the right to manage their own financial affairs. Residents cannot be required to deposit personal funds with the nursing home. If the residents choose to deposit funds with the nursing home, the facility must manage the residents' funds properly. Residents have the right to written quarterly accountings of their funds.

THE RIGHT TO KEEP PERSONAL PROPERTY AND HAVE IT SECURED

All nursing homes are required to have a written policy concerning protection of residents' personal property. If a resident's property is lost, and the nursing home is responsible for the loss, the resident may have a claim against the nursing home to replace the property.

THE RIGHT TO BE FREE FROM ABUSE AND NEGLECT

Residents have the right to be free from physical, sexual, verbal, and mental abuse. Residents have the right to be free from corporal punishment and involuntary seclusion. Residents have the right to be free from neglect. Any failure by the nursing home to provide the resident with necessary services, including those identified in the resident's care plan, constitutes neglect and is a violation of residents' rights. Residents have the right to express complaints and concerns without fear of retaliation.

THE RIGHT TO BE FREE FROM PHYSICAL AND CHEMICAL RESTRAINTS

Residents have the right to be free from unnecessary physical restraints (vest restraints, hand mitts, four point restraints and any and all other physical restraints) and unnecessary chemical restraints (anti-psychotic drugs, sedatives, and any and all other chemical restraints). Restraints are to be used only as treatment for medical symptoms and must be prescribed by a physician. Chemical or physical restraints are not to be used for disciplinary measures, nor may they be used for staff convenience.

THE RIGHT AGAINST UNLAWFUL DISCHARGE OR TRANSFER AND THE RIGHT TO RE-ADMISSION

Due to the seriousness of discharging a resident (the transfer trauma suffered by the resident, the stress undergone by the family members locating a new facility, etc.), the regulations concerning unlawful discharge are very specific and must be followed precisely. A nursing facility may only transfer or discharge a resident for the following reasons:

(I) The transfer or discharge is necessary for the resident's welfare and the resident's needs cannot be met in the facility;

(ii) The transfer or discharge is appropriate because the resident's health has improved sufficiently so the resident no longer needs the services provided by the facility;

(iii) The safety of individuals in the facility is endangered;

(iv) The health of individuals in the facility would otherwise be endangered;

(v) The resident has failed, after reasonable and appropriate notice, to pay for (or to have paid under Medicare or Medicaid) a stay at the facility. For a resident who becomes eligible for Medicaid after admission to a facility, the facility may charge a resident only allowable charges under Medicaid; or

(vi) The facility ceases to operate.

Unless it is an emergency situation, residents must be given written notice 30 days prior to the date of discharge. The "discharge notice" must state the reason for the discharge and the location to which the resident is to be transferred or discharged. The notice must also provide information regarding the right to appeal the discharge.

If a resident is transferred or discharged, the nursing home must develop a discharge plan which provides comprehensive information allowing for continuity of care in the resident's new home. It is never a requirement that family members participate in discharge planning, though nursing homes will often try to force a family to do so.

If a resident requires intermittent hospitalization or therapy outside of the nursing home, for whatever reason, the nursing home must provide the resident with a written copy of its bed hold policy. Specifically, the nursing home must inform the resident how long it will hold the bed and how much the bed hold will cost.

chapter 21

RECOGNIZING ABUSE & NEGLECT

T here are several different types of abuse, some of which are more obvious than others. The following are the types of abuse or violation of rights that often occur. We've also included the signs to look for.

TYPES OF PHYSICAL ABUSE

Physical abuse is perhaps the most obvious, and is usually easier to detect than other forms of abuse. The most common types of physical abuse are:

- Assault — hitting, shaking, pushing, shoving, kicking, burning, choking, scratching, rough-handling, cutting, biting, physically confining, forcibly confining or restraining into a room, a chair, a bed;

- Forcibly feeding;

- Forcibly medicating;

- Over-medicating;

- Sexually molesting;

- Any sexual activity with an adult who is unable to understand or give consent;

- Inflicting pornography, voyeurism, exhibitionism, etc.;

- Control of an adult through the use of threats or intimidation or through the abuse of a relationship of trust;

- Prolonged intervals between an injury and the treatment;

- Frequent changes in doctors.

SIGNS OF PHYSICAL ABUSE

The most common signs of physical abuse are:

- Cuts, scrapes, burns, puncture wounds, marks indicating use of restraints.

- Bruises, discoloration, swelling.

- Difficulty moving.

- Stiffness (trouble walking or sitting). The resident may have been injured internally or suffered broken bones with no external signs.

- Genital infections or pain in the groin area.

Ask the resident what happened. Do they have an explanation for the injury? Is it believable, or do the injuries lead you to a different conclusion?

TYPES OF PSYCHOLOGICAL ABUSE

There are varying degrees of psychological / emotional abuse. Often, this type of abuse is difficult to detect, particularly if you do not witness interactions between the abuser and the resident. The most common types of psychological abuse are:

- Threatening residents (threatening to physically harm residents, threatening to take away their rights, threatening to sell their property, threatening to place them in confinement, threatening to take the residents' power to make choices, etc.);

- Humiliating residents or treating them like children;

- Verbal abuse, insults, name calling;

SIGNS OF PSYCHOLOGICAL ABUSE

The most common signs of psychological abuse are:

- Helplessness;

- Hesitation to talk openly;

- Agitation and/or trouble sleeping;

- Withdrawal and/or depression;

- Implausible stories;

- Fear in the presence of the caregiver;

- Constant deferral to the caregiver, including waiting for the caregiver to answer a question which was posed to the resident;

- Decision-making by the caregiver without deferring or consulting with the resident;

- Resident not accepting/allowing visitors.

TYPES OF NEGLECT

Whether intentional or unintentional, any time residents are left in an unsafe environment or they are not receiving proper care, they are being neglected. The most common types of neglect are:

- Withholding treatment (failing to administer medications, failing to provide physical therapy when needed, not taking to doctor's appointments, etc.);

- Failing to provide assistance with Activities of Daily Living (e.g., toileting, bathing, transferring, eating, etc.), when necessary;

- Withholding food;

- Failing to ensure proper diet;

- Abandoning the resident;

- Failing to provide basic needs - food, clothing, shelter, medicine, medical aids not properly or timely administered.

SIGNS OF NEGLECT

The most common signs of neglect are:

- Malnourishment;

- Dehydration;

- Weight loss;

- Not receiving proper medical care (under or over medicated, missing doctor's appointments, etc.);

- Lacking necessary medical aids (walker, wheelchair, hearing aid, dentures, etc.);

- The presence of pressure sores;

- Inadequate personal hygiene;

- Inadequate and/or inappropriate clothing;

- Inadequate and/or inappropriate supervision;

- Extreme filth of person or surrounding;

- Pest/rodent infestation;

- Offensive odors;

- Inadequate heat, fuel, electricity, refrigeration;

- Untreated physical or mental health problems;

- Abandonment;

- Dilapidated housing condition;

- Soiled bedding.

TYPES OF FINANCIAL EXPLOITATION

Financial abuse, technically called "exploitation," is common among residents and takes on many different forms. Often caregivers coerce residents into selling their property, or giving or loaning them money. Caregivers may obtain the same results through fraud, forgery, and through the crimes of larceny, embezzlement, theft by false pretenses, burglary, false impersonation, and extortion. The most common types of financial abuse are:

- Withholding money belonging to the resident;

- Forcing a resident to sell or give property away;

- Stealing money from a resident;

- Coercing a resident to give away money;

- Borrowing money from a resident and failing to repay it.

SIGNS OF FINANCIAL EXPLOITATION

The most common signs of financial abuse are:

- The resident cannot explain the disappearance of funds in bank account;

- The resident's personal property is missing and he/she has no explanation;

- The resident is suddenly spending a great deal of money;

- The resident suddenly withdraws a lot of money from accounts;

- The resident is unable to pay his or her bills;

- The caregiver does not give the resident an opportunity to speak for him or herself;

- The caregiver is defensive;

- The caregiver gives conflicting accounts of incidents reported by the others (i.e. incidents reported by the resident, family members, friends, neighbors, other health care professionals);

- The caregiver has drug or alcohol problems;

- The caregiver has history of past abuse;

- The caregiver's affection is inappropriate (flirtations, coyness, or other indications that there may be an inappropriate sexual relationship).

chapter *22*

PROTECTION FROM ABUSE AND NEGLECT

O ften residents are not aware they are being abused, perhaps because it has gone on for so long they don't consider it abuse, or perhaps because they suffer a mental illness which renders them incapable of recognizing abuse. Therefore, it is extremely important to be aware of their situation and note any changes that occur. The following are some things that you can do on an ongoing basis to protect the resident.

STAY INFORMED

The resident's health may change, the staffing and administration may change, policies may change, etc. Talk regularly with the resident and establish a relationship with the resident which allows the resident to trust you. Don't ever dismiss what the resident tells you simply because the resident has dementia or some other mental illness which in your mind renders him or her "incompetent."

EDUCATE AND EMPOWER YOURSELF AND THE RESIDENT

Utilize your resources. Resident and Family Councils, for example, are great sources of information inside the nursing home. Outside the nursing home, the Long Term Care Ombudsman is a great resource for advocates. Adult Protective Services is not only reactive, but is a preventive and supportive agency with a wealth of information. Your local Area Agency on Aging is another state agency which provides helpful information, as do outside organizations like the American Association of Retired Persons (AARP) and support groups sponsored by such organizations as the

Alzheimer's Association. In today's world, the Internet is also a vast resource for all kinds of educational information relating to the rights of the elderly. Be sure to share information with the resident whenever possible. Keep in mind that the more control residents have over their lives, the fewer opportunities abusers have to take advantage of them.

ESTABLISH RELATIONSHIPS

Establish relationships with the nursing home staff and with the other residents and their family members. The nursing home staff are with your loved one 24 hours a day. Get to know them. They can be your "eyes and ears" and alert you to possible abuse. Establish a relationship that is both professional and friendly. Do not speak with them only when you are expressing concern or dissatisfaction. Be sure to let them know what you are pleased with.

Other residents and their family members can be both a great support system and a significant source of information. All nursing homes are required to facilitate Resident and Family Councils. These monthly meetings of residents and family members are a way to help one another address shared concerns.

TAKE AN ACTIVE ROLE IN THE RESIDENT'S CARE PLANNING

Attend the monthly care plan meetings (also encourage the resident to attend whenever possible). If the resident has special needs that you are aware of, be sure to let the interdisciplinary team know. Suggest a few ways the resident's needs can be met. Don't be afraid to ask questions. Make sure you understand and agree with the care plan. Obtain a copy of the plan and be sure to follow up with the staff to ensure the care plan is being met.

If you have permission from the resident, periodically review the resident's charts. The first few times you review the chart, ask a staff member to review the chart with you and explain those sections which are confusing to you. Periodically review the resident's financial records, as well (provided the resident has given you permission). Make a list of the residents's personal belongings and periodically check to make sure that all belongings remain accounted for. Many residents also label their belongings for easy identification.

DOCUMENT YOUR CONCERNS

When you visit the resident, keep a journal. Record your observations and keep track of patterns. Note statements made by witnesses. Be sure you record dates and times. Take photographs and videos. When reporting incidents, it helps to have clearly-defined symptoms and conditions. Accuracy is important. If you should ever need to file a complaint, detailed records enable outside parties to have an accurate description of events.

chapter 23

IF YOU SUSPECT ABUSE OR NEGLECT

I f you suspect a nursing home resident is being neglected or abused and the situation requires immediate action, you should speak with the Director of Nursing or the Administrator of the nursing home. In an emergency situation, of course you should call 911. You should also report the incident to your State's Elder Abuse Hotline. Every state has an Elder Abuse Hotline that takes calls from concerned persons who suspect abuse of residents (both domestic and institutional). These Hotlines are generally available 24 hours, 7 days a week, 365 days a year. A page linking to all of the state Elder Abuse Hotlines is available at the National Council on Child Abuse and Family Violence at:

http://tinyurl.com/ElderAbuseHotlines

Information and referral is also available from the national Eldercare Locator, a public service of the U.S. Administration on Aging. Call Toll-Free 1-800-677-1116. This number is available from Monday through Friday 9 AM-8 PM (except U.S. federal holidays).

Another resource is the National Center on Elder Abuse available online at www.elderabusecenter.org and by phone at 202-898-2586. Additionally, all health care workers or nursing home employees who have reason to suspect that an adult has been abused, neglected, or exploited are required to immediately report the incident to the local office of Adult Protective Services.

Problems which are not emergencies and do not rise to the level of abuse or neglect are best resolved at the least formal level. If it is a non-emergency, first speak with the staff person(s) whose job is related to your concern. When you are discussing the problem, cite specific examples. If you are not satisfied with the response, contact the supervisor, the Director of Nursing, or the Administrator of the nursing home. Don't automatically defer to the nursing home employees or assume they are acting within the confines of the law. If a nursing facility staff member tells you "that's the law," demand to know exactly which law he or she means. Similarly, don't automatically defer to a staff member who tells you "these types of things happen," or "nothing can be done." Each facility has a Rights Advisor whose job is to field complaints. Put your concern in writing. The Rights Advisor is required to provide a written response within 30 days of receiving the complaint. If you are not satisfied with the response of the Rights Advisor, your next step is to speak with a Long Term Care Ombudsman. The Long Term Care Ombudsman Program, established in all states under the Older Americans Act, is authorized to investigate and resolve complaints on behalf of nursing home residents. Ombudsmen advocate on behalf of residents and work to bring about changes on local, state, and national levels to ensure quality care.

If you are still not satisfied with the results you have received, or if the abuse is of such a grave nature that you feel the nursing home has violated the law, consult an attorney who specializes in nursing home negligence. If an injury or other violation of the law has occurred, this type of specialized personal injury attorney can advise you as to whether there are potential legal actions that you may be able to successfully pursue.

chapter 24

ESTATE AND INCAPACITY PLANNING

We all know that we will eventually die. At the same time, no one likes to dwell on the prospect of his or her own death. But like everything else in life, failure to plan means planning to fail. But if you, your parents, or other loved ones postpone planning until it is too late, you run the risk that your children or other intended beneficiaries — those you love the most — may not receive all that you would hope, or may not be taken care of in the way you would hope. That is what estate planning is all about — making sure that your loved ones are taken care of when you are gone. All adults need to do estate planning — whether you have fifty thousand or five million dollars, you probably want to distribute your assets in a certain way upon your death, which means you need to do estate planning. However, the best estate plan in the world is meaningless if all of your assets wind up being spent on nursing home care before your death, which is why the information in this chapter must be read and understood in light of all the information contained elsewhere in this book.

WHAT IS AN ESTATE?

We should begin a discussion of estate planning with a review of what "estate" and "estate plan" mean.

An "estate" is everything you own: bank accounts, stocks and bonds, real estate, motor vehicles, retirement plans, life insurance, jewelry, household furniture, etc.

An "estate plan," generally, refers to the means by which your estate is passed on to your loved ones on your death. Estate planning can be accomplished through a variety of methods, including:

- Revocable Living Trusts

- Last Will and Testament / Probate

- Lifetime Gifting

- Joint Ownership

- Beneficiary Designations

- Life Estates

Problems often arise when people don't coordinate all of these methods of passing on their estate. To take just one example, a father's will may say that everything should be equally divided among his children, but if the father creates a joint account with only one of the children "for the sake of convenience," there could be a fight about whether that account should be put back in the pool with the rest of the property.

EXPLANATION OF PROBATE

Without proper incapacity planning documents, your estate will go into living probate if you become incapacitated while you are alive. Dying without a trust, or using a Last Will and Testament as your primary estate planning tool (or dying without a Last Will and Testament), means that your estate will go through post-mortem probate upon your death.

The probate process in most states (both for living probate and post-mortem probate) is an unnecessarily complicated, time-consuming, and expensive process, and can go on for many years.

If you become incapacitated while you are alive and you don't have proper Incapacity Planning documents, then someone will have to go to court to have you declared incompetent. This person will seek to become your legal and financial guardian (sometimes the financial guardian is called a conservator).

To initiate the post-mortem probate process in most states, an Executor nominated in a Last Will and Testament must take the original Will and an original death certificate and make at least one appearance at the probate office to officially "qualify" and be "sworn in" as executor. If you died without a Will or Trust, then someone on your behalf goes to the probate office to become the Administrator of your Estate. Both an Executor of a Will and an Administrator of an Estate are called "Personal Representatives."

Once officially appointed, a Guardian/Conservator and a Personal Representative is accountable to the probate court and is required to prepare and file various legal and financial documents, usually including an initial inventory of the estate and detailed annual accountings showing everything coming in to and going out of the estate. Both a Guardian/Conservator and a Personal Representative must see to it that all assets are accounted for and that any valid debts, expenses, and taxes are paid.

Living probate continues for the lifetime of the incapacitated individual. With post-mortem probate, after a certain period of time from the date of death, the Personal Representative may distribute the remaining assets of the estate.

INCAPACITY PLANNING

To avoid living probate, you need to have incapacity planning document in place. Incapacity planning (which can be done by itself or in connection with your estate planning) involves the signing of three important documents: (1) an Advance Medical Directive, which includes a Living Will and a Medical Power of Attorney; (2) a Durable General Power of Attorney for legal and financial affairs; and (3) a Lifestyle Care Plan. Taken together, these three important documents allow you to decide in advance who will manage your legal, personal, and financial affairs in the event of your disability, and exactly how you will be cared for.

- **Financial Power of Attorney.** Just as a living trust avoids post-mortem probate, a Durable General Financial Power of Attorney authorizes your Agent to act on your behalf and sign your name to financial and/or legal documents. The Financial Power of Attorney is an essential tool if you are unable to carry on your legal and financial affairs due to age, illness, or injury. Having a Financial Power of Attorney will generally avoid the need to go through the time-consuming, expensive, and publicly embarrassing guardianship process, which process is subject to probate court supervision. During the guardianship process, someone goes to court to have you declared mentally or physically incompetent and the court appoints one or more persons to serve as your legal guardian and/or conservator – this is the process of living probate.

- **Health Care Power of Attorney**. A Health Care Power of Attorney (also called a Medical Power of Attorney or an Advance Medical Directive) authorizes another person (called your "Medical Agent"), to make decisions with respect to your medical care in the event that you are physically or mentally unable to do so, as certified by two physicians. This document includes the type of provisions that used to be in what was commonly called a "Living Will," allowing you to indicate your wishes concerning the use of artificial or extraordinary measures to prolong your life artificially in the event of a terminal illness or injury. You will also use this document to indicate your wishes with regard to organ donation, disposition of bodily remains, and funeral arrangements.

- **Lifestyle Care Plan**. A Lifestyle Care Plan is a document that is created by special software that gathers, organizes, stores and disseminates information provided by you in an interview, in order to better serve your future healthcare needs and to guide those who you will depend or for future care. The Lifestyle Care Plan identifies your specific needs, desires, habits and preferences and guides your caregiver in a unique manner. See page 112 for a detailed example of the tremendous benefits of a Lifestyle Care Plan.

ESTATE PLANNING

A well-crafted estate plan could permit your family to save potentially tens or even hundreds of thousands of dollars on taxes, court costs and attorneys' fees. Most importantly, it affords the comfort that your loved ones can mourn your loss without being simultaneously burdened with unnecessary red tape and financial confusion.

Estate planning (including the decision as to whether to use a Will or a Living Trust as your primary estate planning tool), is vitally important for someone who may soon be entering a nursing home.

Just as a good incapacity plan avoids lifetime probate, a good estate plan – one that uses a Revocable Living Trust as the primary estate planning tool – avoids *post-mortem* probate.

REVOCABLE LIVING TRUSTS

A trust is a legal entity which is capable of owning financial assets, real estate, and/or other property.

A **living trust** is a trust that comes into existence during your lifetime, and a Revocable Living Trust is simply a living trust that can be revoked or modified during your lifetime, as opposed to some living trusts that are irrevocable. Using a fully-funded Revocable Living Trust as your primary estate planning tool means that your estate will not go through probate after your death. You create a Revocable Living Trust by signing a contractual document called a "Declaration of Trust" or "Trust Agreement." You are typically the trustee of your own living trust until your death. If you are the initial trustee, then upon your death or disability, a successor trustee whom you have named takes over as trustee of the trust and, after paying any valid debts, expenses, and taxes, distributes the trust assets to or for the benefit of your named beneficiaries or, if called for in the trust, continues to hold the trust assets until the occurrence of a predetermined event.

The main feature of a Revocable Living Trust is that the trustee is not accountable to the court, and therefore not subject to probate. Most people therefore use a Revocable Living Trust as their primary estate planning tool in order to make things easier for their trusted loved ones by avoiding the time and complications of probate. There are also some advantages of using a Revocable Living Trust to consolidate your assets and simplify your finances while you're alive.

chapter 25

HOW TO FIND THE BEST LAWYER

Aging persons and their family members face many unique legal issues. As you have read in this book, the Medicaid program and the myriad legal, financial, care planning, and estate planning issues facing the prospective nursing home resident and family can be particularly complex. If you or a family member needs nursing home care, it is clear that you need expert legal help. Where can you turn for that help? It is difficult for the consumer to identify lawyers who have the training and experience required to provide expert guidance during this most difficult time.

Nursing home planning, Medicaid planning, asset protection planning, and estate planning are all services provided by elder law attorneys. But consumers must be cautious in choosing a lawyer and should always carefully investigate the lawyer's credentials, because anyone can call themselves an elder law attorney.

The most important national credential in the field of elder law is the CELA (Certified Elder Law Attorney) designation. The CELA designation is administered by the Board of Certification of the National Elder Law Foundation, which is the only organization accredited by the American Bar Association to certify lawyers in the specialty area of elder law. Among the numerous criteria required for certification, CELAs must pass a rigorous full-day certification examination and receive favorable peer reviews from at least five other attorneys familiar with their competence and qualifications in elder law. CELAs also must have, during the three years prior to certification: handled at least 60 elder law matters with a specified distribution among 12 different areas of elder law and participated in at least 45 hours of continuing legal education in elder law. You can locate a CELA in your area by visiting www.nelf.org.

The leading professional organization of elder law attorneys is NAELA — the National Academy of Elder Law Attorneys. Though mere membership in the Academy is open to any lawyer and is no guarantee that the attorney is experienced in elder law, membership does at least show that the lawyer has a genuine interest in the field. In addition, NAELA runs several educational sessions each year as well as an Internet discussion group to help attorney members stay current on the latest aspects of elder law. You can find a listing of NAELA members in your area by visiting www.naela.org, which will also tell you if the attorney is a Certified Elder Law Attorney. NAELA suggests you ask lots of questions before selecting an elder law attorney, as you don't want to end up in the office of an attorney who can't help you. Start with the initial phone call. It is not unusual to speak only to a secretary or receptionist during an initial call. Many elder law attorneys do offer free consultations to determine if your issue is something they can help you with. NAELA suggests asking the following questions during your first call: How long has the attorney been in practice? Does his/her practice emphasize a particular area of law? How long has he/she been in this field? What percentage of his/her practice is devoted to elder law? Is there a fee for the first consultation and if so, how much? Given the nature of your problem, what information should you bring with you to the initial consultation?

The answers to your questions will assist you in determining whether that particular attorney has those qualifications important to you for a successful attorney/client relationship. If you have a specific legal issue that requires immediate attention, be sure to inform the office of this during the initial telephone conversation.

In addition to looking for attorneys with the CELA designation and who are members of NAELA, you may want to seek recommendations from any friends and family members who have received professional help with elder law and/or nursing home issues (who did they use and were they satisfied with the services they received?). Hospital social workers, discharge planners, accountants, financial professionals, and other attorneys can also be good sources of recommendations.

Most states and many local bar associations have formal lawyer referral services that can refer you to an elder law attorney. Be aware, however, that many bar association referral services allow new or inexperienced attorneys to join and do not limit the number of attorneys who may join, so if you use a referral service be sure to check how it operates.

The Internet can be another good source of information about elder law attorneys. There are several well-known services that offer peer-review ratings of attorneys. The most reputable of such services are:

- Martindale-Hubbell Law Directory, at www.martindale.com. Look for an Elder Law attorney who is rated AV, which is the highest rating.

- SuperLawyers.com lists the top 5% of attorneys in each state in each practice area.

- Avvo.com rates attorneys on a scale of 1 through 10. Look for an Elder Law attorney with a rating of 10.

- Best Lawyers – www.bestlawyers.com also lists an elite group of attorneys who have been voted into membership by their peers.

Obviously, you can also find out a lot about an attorney from his or her own Web site.

In general, a lawyer who devotes a substantial part of his or her practice to elder law and nursing home planning should have more knowledge and experience to address the issues properly. Don't hesitate to ask the lawyer what percentage of his practice involves nursing home planning. Or you may want to ask how many new nursing home planning cases the law office handles each month. There is no correct answer. But there is a good chance that a law office that assists with one or two nursing home placements a week is likely to be more up-to-date and knowledgeable than an office that helps with one or two placements a year.

Ask whether the lawyer is involved with committees or local or state bar organizations that have to do with elder law or estate planning? If so, has the lawyer held a position of authority on the committee? Does the lawyer lecture on elder law and/or estate planning? If so, to whom? If the lawyer lectures to the public, you might try to attend one of the seminars. This should help you decide if this lawyer is right for you. If the lawyer is asked to speak at educational seminars to other lawyers about elder law and nursing home planning, that is a very good sign that the lawyer is considered to be knowledgeable by people who ought to know.

In the end, follow your instincts and choose an attorney who knows this area of the law, who is committed to helping others, and who will listen to you and the unique desires and needs of you and your family.

chapter 26

CONCLUSION

As you have seen, there are numerous strategies that you can use to qualify for Medicaid and still preserve — for yourself and, if desired, for your heirs — some or all of the assets you've spent a lifetime building. As explained in chapter 15, these strategies are legal. They are moral. They are ethical. Medicaid planning is no different from income tax planning (trying to find all of the proper and legal deductions that you are entitled to) or estate tax planning (trying to plan your estate to minimize the amount of estate tax that will be paid). However, as this book has explained numerous times, Medicaid planning requires a great deal of extremely complicated knowledge about the Medicaid system and its complex regulations. You need to work with an experienced Elder Law Attorney, preferably a Certified Elder Law Attorney, who knows the rules and can advise you properly.

In the previous pages, I've explained how to find the right nursing home, how to get the best care there, and how to pay for care without going broke. I've also explained that you can start looking at www.medicare.gov/NHCompare, where you can search for nursing homes by City and State and easily determine whether a given nursing home accepts Medicaid (most do).

Once you've determined which facilities you want to tour, then you can use the Evaluation Tool on page 24 to help you compare them. Other helpful resources can be found in the Appendix.

Good luck to you and your family as you embark on this challenging journey of transition.

APPENDIX – NATIONAL RESOURCES

AARP
Toll-Free Nationwide: 888-OUR-AARP
www.aarp.org
A national membership organization whose purpose is to enhance the quality of life for persons over age 50, promote independence, and improve the image of aging.

Alzheimer's Association
www.alz.org
Toll Free Nationwide 24/7 Helpline: 1-800-272-3900
The Alzheimer's Association is the premier source of information and support for Americans with Alzheimer's disease and related disorders.

Eldercare Locator
Toll Free: 800-677-1116
www.eldercare.gov
A public service of the U.S. Administration on Aging designed to help identify community resources for seniors and their caregivers anywhere in the U.S.

Medicare Nursing Home Compare Web Site
Online nursing home comparison tool.
www.medicare.gov/NHCompare

National Association of Professional Geriatric Care Managers
Telephone: 520-881-8008
www.caremanager.org
A group of professionals trained in the field of human services who are dedicated to promoting the advancement of dignified care for older adults. Members are certified or licensed at the independent practice level.

ABOUT THE AUTHOR

Evan Farr, Certified Elder Law Attorney, is the creator of the Living Trust Plus™ Asset Protection System used by dozens of Estate Planing and Elder Law Attorneys around the U.S., and Evan is widely recognized as one of the foremost experts in the Country in the field of Medicaid Asset Protection and related Trusts. Evan has been quoted or cited as an expert by numerous sources, including the Washington Post, Newsweek Magazine, Trusts & Estates Magazine, The American Institute of Certified Public Accountants, and the American Bar Association, and has been featured as a guest speaker on numerous radio shows, including WTOP and Washington Post Radio. Evan received a degree in Psychology from the University of Pennsylvania in 1984 and his law degree from the College of William & Mary in 1987.

Evan is AV-Rated by Martindale-Hubbell, is named in the Best Lawyers in America, and has been named by SuperLawyers.com as one of the top 5% of Elder Law and Estate Planning attorneys in Virginia every year since 2007, and in the Washington, DC Metro Area every year since 2008. In 2011, Evan was named by Washingtonian Magazine as one of the top attorneys in the DC Metropolitan area, by Northern Virginia Magazine as one of the top attorneys in the Northern Virginia area, and by Newsweek Magazine as one of the top attorneys in the country. In 2012 Evan was named by Virginia Lawyers Weekly as one of the year's "Leaders in the Law," recognizing Evan as an attorney who sets the standard for other attorneys in the state.

Evan is a nationally renowned Best-Selling author and frequent educator of attorneys across the U.S. As an expert to the experts, Evan has educated tens of thousands of attorneys across the country through speaking and writing for organizations such as his own Elder Law Institute for Training and Education (ELITE), the National Academy of Elder Law Attorneys (NAELA), the American Law Institute-American Bar Association (ALI-ABA), the National Business Institute (NBI), the Virginia Academy of Elder Law Attorneys (VAELA), the Virginia Bar Association (VBA), Virginia Continuing Legal Education (Virginia CLE), and the District of Columbia Bar Association. His numerous publications include a Best-Selling book, *Protect and Defend*, as well as numerous articles that have appeared in the popular press, and numerous scholarly publications for the legal profession, including two legal treatises published by the American Law Institute in affiliation with the American Bar Association: *Planning and Defending Asset Protection Trusts* and *Trusts for Senior Citizens*.

Evan has served in numerous leadership positions for local and Statewide Bar Associations and Sections, including: President of the Virginia Academy of Elder Law Attorneys; Chair of the Virginia Bar Association Elder Law Section; Chair of the Fairfax Bar Association Elder Law Section; and Co-Chair of the Fairfax Bar Association Wills, Trusts & Estates Section.

Using a holistic and proprietary approach, Evan and the Farr Law Firm use a vast knowledge, understanding, and deep respect of the elderly to help their elderly clients and their families preserve dignity, quality of life, and financial security, often by protecting assets in order to become eligible for Medicaid and Veterans Aid and Attendance benefits.

Virginia has no procedure for approving certifying organizations.

Made in the USA
Columbia, SC
26 October 2017